Seven Days *of* Spiritual Evolution

T0350628

SEVEN DAYS
of Spiritual Evolution

THE GENESIS *of* PERSONAL TRANSFORMATION

E. Kent Rogers

SWEDENBORG FOUNDATION

West Chester, Pennsylvania

Library of Congress Cataloging-in-Publication Data

Names: Rogers, E. Kent, author.
Title: Seven days of spiritual evolution : the genesis of
    personal transformation / E. Kent Rogers.
Description: West Chester, Pennsylvania : Swedenborg
    Foundation, 2018. | Includes bibliographical references.
Identifiers: LCCN 2018026436| ISBN 9780877853091 (pbk. :
    alk. paper) | ISBN 0877853096 (pbk. : alk. paper)
Subjects: LCSH: Bible. Genesis, I--Commentaries. | New
    Jerusalem Church--Doctrines.
Classification: LCC BS1235.53 .R64 2018 | DDC 230/.94--dc23
LC record available at https://lccn.loc.gov/2018026436

Edited by John Connolly
Design and typesetting by Karen Connor

The Scripture quotations contained herein are from the New
Revised Standard Version Bible, copyright © 1989 by the Division
of Christian Education of the National Council of the Churches of
Christ in the USA, and are used by permission. All rights reserved.

Printed in the United States of America

Swedenborg Foundation
320 North Church Street
West Chester, PA 19380
www.swedenborg.com

CONTENTS

FROM *SECRETS OF HEAVEN*

Our outer self can survive only from and through our inner self, and our inner self can survive only from and through heaven. Heaven cannot survive on its own, only from the Lord, the only one who subsists on his own. . . .

The whole of nature unites to shape a person's exterior. That is why the ancients called a person a microcosm.

Just as the outer self is formed in the image of the whole world, then, the inner self is formed in the image of everything in heaven—that is, in the image of heavenly and spiritual qualities radiating from the Lord, which compose and contain heaven. . . . These qualities are innately so abundant and extraordinary that the tongue cannot possibly describe one millionth of them. . . .

When [angels] appear before one's inner eye (as they have before mine), [they] move one's inmost depths by their presence alone. Love for the Lord and charity for their neighbor pour from them with penetrating effect, while the ramifications of love and charity—the elements of faith—gleam from them with touching effect. . . .

This evidence now shows that the spiritual world unites with the physical world in the human being. Consequently the spiritual world flows into the physical world in such a tangible way in us that we can sense it if we simply pay attention. . . .

The interaction of the soul with the body . . . is communication between the spiritual attributes of heaven and the physical attributes of the world. Clearly the communication relies on spiritual inflow, or influence, and varies in keeping with the union [between inner and outer].

This communication . . . is unknown today, because people attribute anything and everything to nature. They know nothing about the spiritual realm, which is now so remote that when they think about it, they see it as a nonentity.

Here is what spiritual influence is like: The Lord's divinity exerts an influence on every angel, every spirit, and every person on earth. That is how he governs everyone, not only in a comprehensive way but also in the smallest details. (§§6056; 6057:1–2, 3; 6058)

ACKNOWLEDGMENTS

To all my clients—past, present, and future—you have richly blessed my life in sharing yours, in allowing me to offer a hand and a word, and in giving me the opportunity to walk a ways with you along the beautiful paths of psychological and spiritual progress.

And to Shovha, thank you for holding my hand and whispering your words to me when I could not see the way. I am so grateful to share this amazing journey together with you.

ooooo

Imagine having the onerous position of finishing a home designed and roughly built by a finicky architect. You add the trim, sand the cabinets, apply the paint, and tile the floor, only to have the architect come back the next month with "a new plan"! The kitchen wall needs to be moved out ten feet; we are doing away with the cabinets; and the tiles "have to match the fall colors outside." "But, uh, a month ago you wanted it to match the summer colors outside," you think to yourself. The architect also complains about things taking too long, despite the fact that most often he is responsible for delays in progress. Oh, and the walls need to be a different color. That is pretty much what John Connolly had to deal with as the editor of this book. Brother John, I owe you tremendous thanks and credit for the completion of this book. Thank you for your patience, expertise, and thoughtful additions to the content. It was a privilege working with you.

ABOUT THIS BOOK

Many years ago, I had what I consider to be a spiritual experience. While meditating, Genesis 1–11 began to play through my mind in succession, almost as if I were watching a stylized silent cinematic summary of the stories. As this film rolled on, each story was accompanied by its *inner meaning*—a meaning that related to a person's individual spiritual development. Ever since then, I have wanted to write a book that expresses the ideas of this experience. This book fulfills that goal, at least up through Genesis 1. I hope one day to write a book that describes an inner meaning of the Bible beyond that point.

This wonderful experience has roots that reach deep into the rich soil of the Christian tradition in which I was raised, one based on the theology of Emanuel Swedenborg (1688–1772)—a Swedish scientist, philosopher, and visionary. In the 1700s, Swedenborg wrote extensively about an inner meaning hidden within the Bible—in much the same way that a deeper meaning is held within a parable or allegorical tale. The Word, he explained, is about our spiritual lives: the wars are the battles we wage against our inner demons; different places represent our many general states of mind; and the different biblical characters represent the various elements of thought and volitional life that together comprise our consciousness. These ideas were revealed to him while meditating on the Word.

In fact, across the recent fifteen-volume New Century Edition translation of *Secrets of Heaven*, Swedenborg presents the inner meaning of both Genesis and half of Exodus. My goal with this book is to offer an easy-to-understand explanation of an inner meaning within the Creation story, one that has practical relevance for our times. There is a great deal of overlap in how I interpret the inner meaning of the text and what Swedenborg explained. However, there are some differences of interpretation that echo my own experiences in exploring both the written Word and the other revelation, life. Just as different-colored gems receive and reflect sunlight in different ways, so each mind will receive and reflect the light of God in different ways.

As it is difficult for me to accept spiritual or religious truth without both recognizing its veracity with my own mind and seeing its practical value, I have spent a good deal of time since my youth searching for meaning and truth. This has included both formal and informal study of many different traditions, including Buddhism, Hinduism, Taoism, liberation theology, evangelical Christianity, Swedenborgianism, Western philosophy, and psychology. All of these traditions have offered valuable insights; and along with my personal spiritual experiences, these insights exert influence on how I understand God, life, and the human condition.

This book is intended to be used as a tool for anyone, Christian and non-Christian alike, interested in working toward spiritual development. I have tried to be ecumenical and at the same time write from my own personal faith. Just as a tree's structure is spread out at the roots, converges into a trunk, and then spreads out once again into a canopy of branches, my search for meaning spread roots in many directions and converged to become my personal faith. My hope is that the value of this book can spread out like branches to serve a wide variety of people, regardless of their faith. As you will see, most of the ideas offered have psychological application and describe universally experienced states of mind. Faith isn't about drawing lines in the sand or judging others; it's about learning how to love others and to love God.

To avoid any misunderstandings about what Christianity means to me, I will explain the basics of my faith. I do not believe in the idea of Jesus as a sacrifice either to appease an angry Father or to fulfill the need for a blood offering required by God's justice in relation to sin. Such ideas about Jesus have become so common that "Christianity" can sometimes be equated with this type of understanding. In fact, the doctrine of Jesus being a blood sacrifice to fulfill divine justice didn't fully come into being until Calvin, more than a thousand years after Jesus walked the earth. Such a doctrine bends focus away from Jesus's life and onto his death, emphasizing his literal blood rather than the spirit of his life's message—namely, that we are loved and that we are to love. This living message of love exemplified in his life, his teachings, and his willingness to die is the lifeblood, not the literal blood, shed to save us. And our salvation is achieved by adopting such love into our lives, letting it animate us so that we may become loving beings. Saying "I believe" but not adopting a life of love affects little if anything, whereas living a life of godly love—even in the absence of saying these words—reveals the essential character of Jesus, which is selfless love. God is love, and God's love is salvation. Because God loves us, he wanted to be with us, even if that meant having to die.

It is not difficult to see that love is heaven; it is salvation. Selfless love is what frees our spirit, brings us peace, and brings us happiness. For me, knowing and following Jesus has proven to be the most direct path to a state of love. I believe that there is only one person of God and that Jesus is the face and hands of God.

Throughout this book, I will use either *God* or *the Divine* for those less personal and more conceptual discussions of God, and I will use either *Lord* or *Jesus* when I am relating my own personal experience or when I want to stress an intimate relationship with a human God, a friend who understands us and loves us. Nevertheless, I believe that God and Jesus are one, just as mind and body are one.

That Jesus is one with the Father and that salvation is not obtained by words of faith in a sacrifice but by the reception of God's love into our lives are both foundational ideas of the theology found in Swedenborg's writings.

ooooo

Each chapter of this book provides the reader with suggested practices. Performing these activities can help actualize the concepts that are described throughout the chapters and make them useful in everyday life. It is also recommended that you record your experiences and observations as a way of helping to chart your development. The suggested practices sections include tasks that help to cultivate awareness in daily activities, meditations, exercises, and suggested questions for pondering and/or discussion. With the meditations, note that time indications (e.g., **[Pause for 1 minute]**) are approximations and that italicized text indicates material to be recited—either aloud, if in a group setting, or silently, if by oneself. For your convenience, MP3 versions of these meditations can be found at www.swedenborg.com.

The particular tasks and extended practices that I suggest draw on many elements of my own experience. I have participated in a number of spiritual growth groups that have proven very valuable. My degree and practice in mental health counseling have offered many practical methods for improving ways of thinking and behaving; and my personal exploration of meditation and mindfulness techniques has complemented these methods.

Since we often gain a great deal from sharing one another's ideas and experiences, this book is best used in the context of a group. If you are able to gather with others, each chapter should be read within a day or two after the group meets so that the time between meetings can be devoted to the practices. The introduction should be read by everyone before the first meeting. Alternatively, if you are unable to meet with a group or you prefer working alone, the tools in this book may be used independently to good effect. As spiritual evolution does not happen overnight, you may spend as little or as much time as you need working through each of the days.

INTRODUCTION

*[The] effort constantly to experience the whole of one's inner life is what
has lent every great reading of the Bible the authority that speaks from
the unknown in the universe to the unknown in myself.*

— From Jacob Needleman's foreword to Maurice Nicoll's *The New Man*

Whether we are ready or not, we have no choice but to live
the journey that is our life. It would definitely be nice to know
in advance a bit more about what this marvelous and terrible
journey entails, but we are given no information about most of
the earthly events we will experience. I believe we *are*, however,
given a rich itinerary for the spiritual path that we will simultaneously travel as life unfolds. And as a result of my own extensive study and personal spiritual experiences, I believe that the
Bible is this itinerary.

The premise of the book you are currently holding is simple:
the Bible as a whole is a parable that details our progressive
walk with and toward God. The spiritual cannot be adequately
expressed within the boundaries of logic and the intellect, so
symbolic story makes sense as a medium for its expression.
Since God is beyond the boundaries of human reason, the best
our mind can do is point the way. I believe that the stories of
the Bible provide a fuller expression of how the Divine interacts

with us than do straightforward rational explanations. The wise men of the East discover the star over Bethlehem, which represents intellectual concepts of God, but it is up to us to progress toward the dawning of divine love with our mind, with our heart, and with how we live.

A number of clues in the Bible suggest its stories are something other than a literal description. Scholars have concluded, for example, that the number of Israelites leaving Egypt simply can't be true on a literal level. And there is actually no evidence that the Israelites were ever slaves in Egypt or that there was an exodus at all. The description of the origin of the human race from Adam and Eve doesn't hold up in light of the fact that their children, Seth and Cain, went out and found wives. So perhaps the point of these stories isn't to describe the details of a literal history but to explain spiritual phenomena that take place within us.

The Bible also contains internal references that imply a depth of meaning beyond the words themselves. In the story of the walk to Emmaus (Luke 24:13–35), for example, we read that "beginning with Moses and all the prophets, [Jesus] interpreted . . . the things about himself in all the scriptures," which reveals that under the surface meaning of the Old Testament is a hidden message describing his own birth, life, death, and resurrection. Another such clue can be found in tying together two statements that are made in the New Testament: "In the beginning was the Word, and the Word was with God, and the Word was God" (John 1:1) and "The Word became flesh and lived among us" (John 1:14). Here, an equation between Jesus and the whole Word of God, or the Bible, is established. Similarly, in Matthew 5:17, we read that Jesus did not "come to abolish the law or the prophets . . . but to fulfill [them]." In Mark 4:34, we read that Jesus "did not speak . . . except in parables." If Jesus is the Word of God, and he speaks only using parables, then the Word of God speaks to us by means of parable.

That the Bible has a deeper meaning, though, is not an entirely new or alien idea. The Promised Land is understood by many to be symbolic of heaven. The number forty is known as a symbol of temptation, and the number seven indicates holiness. Several symbolic interpretations of the books of Daniel and Revelation have been suggested. What *is* new, at least to most people, is the idea that the entire Bible, from beginning to end, is a single parable. Such a vision of the Bible was first offered more than two-and-a-half centuries ago by Emanuel Swedenborg. One of his many profound ideas is that the Bible from beginning to end employs these same material symbols to create, in addition to its surface and well-understood meaning, an allegorical meaning that reveals the process of our spiritual transformation in God. He offers that, unbeknownst to its authors, the Bible was guided by the Divine to describe our spiritual journey using corresponding stories and representations from the natural realm.

Swedenborg explained how the Bible has several simultaneous layers of meaning—one describing our personal journey, a deeper one describing the spiritual progression of the human race, and the deepest describing the spiritual journey that Jesus experienced from the time of his birth through to his resurrection. According to Swedenborg, all three of these progressions parallel each other because the life of Jesus is the source of all human life, and it is Jesus alone who fights and wins in our battle against selfishness and its resulting harm. Therefore, the spiritual progress of each of us is a finite, limited, and imperfect recapitulation of Jesus's spiritual progression—the progression of pure divine, selfless love—a spiritual fractal of life. This divine love faces every form of temptation to abandon love for the sake of selfish ends; and ultimately, it always succeeds in resisting and in turn conquering all forms of evil and so also all delusion arising from selfishness. This will be discussed in greater detail later in the book.

While I have studied Swedenborg's works in depth and my thoughts are greatly influenced by his, I've never been content to just accept what I am told as true. If the Bible is indeed a single parable, I want to see it for myself. Only then does it become genuinely meaningful and personal. For me, the most compelling evidence that the Bible is a parable is what I see when I search for its inner meaning. Below its surface lies a coherent, consistent message that not only offers light to my mind but also touches my heart with a joyful feeling of the presence of God. In fact, I consider this coherency and consistency to be the sufficient and necessary criteria for the validity of an allegorical interpretation. I also see the unity and continuity of meaning to be strong evidence that the Bible was actually designed to be understood in this light. Finally, the personal blessing and spiritual guidance offered by the inner meaning are pragmatic evidence of God's presence there— good fruit comes only from a good tree.

The Bible is couched in histories, but it is not a history book; it tells stories of interesting characters, but it is not about these figures; it touches on matters that overlap with scientific pursuits, but it is not a science manual. And in the same way, while the Bible has a literal meaning, it is not to be understood as primarily literal. As the Lord's parables were symbolic, the Bible reveals itself as a symbolic story that carries important information about God's true nature and about our true relationship with God. Also, since its holiness is held in symbolic meaning, I can believe in the Word of God fully and not have to reject the findings of science or archaeology.

This is not to say that there are no occasions for understanding the Bible in a literal way. There are many statements made in the Bible that are clearly to be understood on a literal level. As I see it, while the overall narrative is symbolic, literal statements are frequently offered within its course. Some examples of such statements include "Love one another as I have loved you" (John 15:12); "Love your enemies and pray for those who persecute you" (Matthew 5:44); and, of course, the Ten Commandments of the Old Testament (Exodus 20:2–17). Indeed, these face-value statements serve as guideposts in working to understand inner content—*does this inner meaning support the ideals of refraining from harmful behaviors, loving others, and loving the Lord?*

God is infinite, and we are finite individuals, so I believe that God speaks to all of us uniquely, meeting us where we are. We are all going to be in different states of mind at different times, so the same story will offer each of us something particular to that state. In fact, because our states of mind change with time, we will see something new of God's communication over time.

Knowing Our Destination

I believe that the inner meaning of the Bible can offer us great help in our journey through life. First, it can help us to know our destination. When I moved to Nepal, I needed legal assistance to register New Life Children's Home with the government. After an initial meeting with Bhumi, our lawyer, he dropped me off on the corner of a busy road called Putali Sadak and instructed me to meet him at that same spot at one o'clock on the following day. At that time, street numbers were not in use in Nepal; in fact, many streets didn't even have names. By the next day, I couldn't remember the exact location. Since I didn't know my way around Kathmandu, I caught a taxi, hoping the cabbie would recognize the place if I were able to offer him something resembling its real name. After driving around for an hour trying to find the right corner, I gave up. While it was a memorably frustrating experience for me, I'm sure it was a memorably lucrative excursion for the cabbie.

It's hard to make a meeting when we don't know where we are going. Similarly, if we don't know our spiritual destination, we aren't going to get there very quickly. Even if we know that our goal is the kingdom of heaven, we'll waste a lot of time driving up the wrong roads unless we have some good solid information about who God really is. The inner meaning of the Bible has provided me with invaluable information about God's nature. Obviously, there are as many different views of God as there are those who seek God. I don't claim to offer the only true or the best view of God. But after years of earnest searching, what I do have to offer is a vision of God that works for me, that makes sense to me, and that might prove useful to others.

As we will see, the spiritual message within the Creation story offers us a vision of a compassionate, human God who hovers over the surface of our minds until we are ready for his light. He is a God who leads us up into ever-more-abundant life until we eventually arrive at a state of deep spiritual peace. This is not a God of judgment but one of universal evolution. There is no need for blood sacrifice. Instead, there is a progressive awakening away from our lower states of mind up toward higher states of mind that bring us into increasing awareness of God's pure love for us all. Entering into the life of this divine and human love is our destination.

Knowing the Way

In any journey, having a destination is not enough; we also need to know the path that leads us there. Learning to understand the Word of God as a parable of our spiritual journey reveals both the destination and the path. When I was about sixteen years old, I decided to hop on my new bicycle and head west through Philadelphia toward Lancaster County. The plan was to go as far as I could in four hours. I had a destination—Lancaster—but I had no specific set of directions or path to guide me on my journey. All I knew is that I had to go west. It wasn't long before I became lost in a run-down area of Philly.

Fortunately, I noticed that I was near a bus stop, so when the next SEPTA bus pulled up, I asked the driver for some help.

"Where you trying to get?"

"West."

"Well, you need to go this-a-way," he said, pointing toward an intimidating street. "But don't be goin' there—it ain't safe. C'mon," he said, "stick your bike in here and I'll get you where you need to go." I had no money, but he still gave me a lift.

God surely sends his angels, like this driver, to help us reach our destination without harm, but if we have good directions that show us what to expect on the journey, how to avoid danger, and how to navigate through difficult situations, we can spare ourselves a lot of trouble and arrive in a happy place earlier rather than later. With experience, we may also find that we are able to guide other people through the troubled neighborhoods of their own minds and on toward their spiritual destinations.

If we know the challenges that lie ahead of us, we will be less anxious and more prepared when the time comes to actually face them. Knowing that someone has arranged our travels for us and that everything is going according to schedule helps us to loosen up and enjoy the ride. We learn to relax into a sense of adventure and excitement about the journey. I used to be a very anxious person, but in having come to see and feel God's love and guidance—a message that I see in the inner meaning of the Word—I feel much less anxiety.

Knowing where we're going and how to get there also helps us to actively apply ourselves to the plan—not just to get there more efficiently but to feel that unique and intimate relationship with God that is captured by the expression "God is my co-pilot." Knowing our destination helps us to be an actual co-pilot and not just a passenger who watches the world go by. Somewhat paradoxically, then, we can relax and enjoy life more while at the same time being more active in its course.

The symbolic meaning of Genesis 1 offers a very clear communication about what our journey is going to look like and how we can actively participate to expedite the process. It is an exciting adventure!

Knowing Where We Begin

No less important than knowing our destination and route is our knowledge of where we begin. We know our destination, and we have a fantastic map; but if we have no idea from where we are starting, then the map won't be of any use to us and our arrival time will recede in the distance. When understood as a parable of our spiritual journey, the Bible reveals to us where we begin; it gives us a "You Are Here" arrow on the map of life. At the risk of revealing my navigational naïveté, here is yet another story of a traveling mishap. When I was about twenty-one years old, I found myself in beautiful San Francisco during a spring break tour with the Grinnell Singers. Our beloved director John Stuhr-Rommereim was an aficionado of all things Russian, especially Russian music (I still consider it a great privilege to have been given the opportunity to sing Rachmaninoff's *All Night Vigil*), and so invited us to attend a Russian Orthodox service with him. The cathedral was as gorgeous as the four-part chants that drifted down from the loft. Sadly, this beauty wasn't able to outweigh the discomfort of having to stand for the entire service or the tedium of understanding not a single word of the Russian language that was both sung and spoken (our director had assured us the service would be in English).

Surreptitiously, I slipped out the door into the shimmering freedom of morning sunlight. I felt immediately closer to God. I had about three hours to get back to the hotel for our warm-up before the afternoon concert, so I headed out on foot in the direction from which we had come. As I walked on and on, my confidence in knowing where I was going began to wane.

The neighborhoods became progressively rougher, until I was looking at broken windows, boarded-up buildings, needles on the sidewalk, and graffiti. Noticing some graffiti on a boarded-up building that read "Good riddance crack-heads," I regretted my decision to navigate back on my own. Then, after taking a few more steps forward, I heard the thumping of an electric bass and drum set. Some happy chords floated above the rhythm section as I got closer to the source. I looked around for a music shop but saw none. When I got to the corner, I saw a Baptist church out from which the clear, joyful sounds of gospel music poured. The music made me happy, and I was compelled to enter. Smiling faces greeted me, and an usher escorted me to a pew on the left that was about halfway up the aisle. Sliding into my spot, I began clapping and, as best I could, singing with the others. Despite being the only white person in the swaying crowd, I felt totally welcomed and right at home—I loved the passion and spirit. This was my kind of service!

The preacher began to speak. I was aware of the time, but I wanted to stay as long as possible. He told us that we were in for a special treat—a guest was coming, a famous speaker. People began to call out, "All right!" "Lay it on us!" The preacher went on, building up the suspense and fervently informing us of how powerful and wonderful was the man who we were about to meet. People were calling out more and more until everyone was standing, clapping, and hooting loudly. I couldn't believe my luck! Who was this going to be, the Rev. Jesse Jackson? Finally, the preacher told us: Jesus, the Christ. The room burst into even louder clapping and cheers. I stayed a little bit longer but then had to slip out of the service (for the second time in one Sunday!) to get back for rehearsal.

The primary problem of this eventful excursion was that I didn't know where I had begun my walk. I was also suffering under the delusion that I could find my way back to the right place, by the right time, and without much trouble; in that sense, I didn't know where I was at all. It was when I saw the spray-painted message "Good riddance crack-heads" that I woke up to the truth and realized where I was—in a worrisome neighborhood. Just a few paces on from that realization, I was ushered into a wonderful moment that I will always cherish. To this day, that was the most lively and spirited service that I have ever attended.

This story demonstrates how we can only really be found by God when we wake up to the fact that we are lost. And as the inner meaning of the first day of Creation will show, we can't see the light until we realize we're in the dark. We need to know where we are starting out, and sometimes that means coming to the realization that we have no idea at all where we are.

I believe that Genesis 1 functions as the brochure that outlines in briefest form the itinerary of our spiritual travels. It is the "abstract" of the Bible, capturing the symbolic message that develops in greater detail throughout the rest of the Word of God. This first chapter of Genesis reveals the basics of how the Lord evolves our spirit. The rest of the Bible expands upon this summary, showing us all the suffering that we'll endure, all the obstacles that we'll face, and all the joys and wonders that we'll experience within our spiritual journey. The Word also shows us that God helps us; time and again, the Lord meets us where we are and delivers us from the false ideas and selfish desires that assail us.

I have sometimes deeply felt and caught glimpses of the fact that God guides us all toward goodness by his infinite love. These things have radically altered both my outlook and the course of my life. If God hadn't allowed me to feel his beautiful love for all people, I'd never have found myself running an orphanage in Nepal, marrying my wonderful wife Shovha, or having the privilege of being a father. Seeing a grander pattern that arcs through all experience, feeling a deeper meaning flowing under the surface of our mundane perceptions, and knowing a divine purpose with which we participate all grant us a higher vision and the capacity to endure troubles without growing weak. As the beautiful words in Isaiah suggest, "those who wait for the Lord shall renew their strength, they shall mount up with wings like eagles, they shall run and not be weary, they shall walk and not faint" (40:31). Feeling these things certainly doesn't mean we no longer experience inner struggle or encounter external problems; it does mean, however, that we have a very different experience of those hurdles. Near the end of his life, Jesus explained that the strife and sorrows of this world are like the pain of childbirth: "When [a woman's] child is born, she no longer remembers the anguish because of the joy of having brought a human being into the world" (John 16:21). The newborn child can be seen to mean the birth of our spiritual awakening. The internal meaning of the Bible helps fulfill these comforting words.

The Language of Parables

Understanding the Word as a parable can be compared to understanding a language. The objects, people, and events that populate the literal meaning of the Word are like the letters and words that make up the form of a written and spoken language, whereas the spiritual components of the Bible's inner meaning represent the meanings of those letters and words. We can recognize the letters and even pronounce the words, but we need to find out what the words, sentences, and passages mean. We need a system for interpreting the Word as a parable, a system that is consistent yet adaptable to context.

For a symbolic understanding of the Bible to make sense, it must meet three criteria. First, the deeper meaning of the symbols should fit those symbols in such an elegant way that when one hears the meaning, the mind immediately recognizes its sensibility.

Second, the symbols as presented in the sequence offered by the literal stories should be easily interpreted into a continuous, coherent spiritual message. Thus, not only must the meaning of each symbol make intuitive and logical sense, but the meaning of the strings of symbols as they are laid out in the Bible must also make sense. Having a set of symbols that translates into gibberish is pointless, even if the individual meaning of each symbol makes sense. Think of Chinese pictographs. The meaning held within each symbol may make sense, but the actual meaning is created only when the symbols are properly ordered. The literal sense of the Bible sets the order. If that order proves meaningful on the symbolic level, it suggests that the choice of words and the ordering of those words have been selected for the sake of an interior meaning and that we've discovered the key to unlocking deep secrets held within the Bible. We've found the Rosetta Stone of the true message within the Bible.

Third, the meaning yielded from a symbolic interpretation of the Bible must be useful. There is little point in discovering an inner message if there is no derived benefit to human welfare. This secret meaning must yield an improved life. It may lend itself to psychological or spiritual healing; it may lead to repentance; it may inspire an increase in acts of kindness and selfless love; or it may open up a more profound sense of God's love and presence in our lives. If any of these blessings come out of our understanding of a symbolic interpretation, then we can know without a doubt that such an interpretation is good.

Swedenborg says that there are two realms, a spiritual and a material, and that they are intimately connected: each aspect of the physical universe is an analogous expression of a spiritual reality. The syntax of this new symbolic language is founded on the idea that the spiritual and material realms parallel one another, that the physical is a reflection of the spiritual. A few examples can help shed light on the matter. The phrase *shed light* is itself a very good example. The analogy between light, a physical manifestation, and truth, a spiritual one, is so common that we don't even realize we are speaking in a language of symbols. *Clear* and *clarity* are words that indicate transparency in the physical realm. We use them symbolically to describe a mental state of accurate perception brought about by the light of truth. *Light* is perhaps the clearest example of a term that is pregnant with symbolic meaning. When we read about light in the Word of God, the Lord is talking to us about the spiritual light of truth and understanding, not about physical light.

If light is truth, then we can *see* how our physical vision, our sense of sight, parallels our spiritual vision, our ability to understand. When we say, "I see," we really mean that we understand. We see light in the world around us just as we understand meaning in the world within. Our spirit possesses the same functions that we find in the body. Let's look at hearing, for example. In colloquial English, if we wish to sympathize with how someone is feeling, we say, "I hear you." When we expect someone to obey us, we say, "Do you hear me?" (What we really mean when we say that is: "Align your will with mine!") In both cases, the underlying message is one of emotional congruence. It is no coincidence, then, that music is essentially the art of harmony, of aligning tones; nor is it a coincidence that most of us find much more of an emotional experience in listening to music than we do in looking at visual art. If the eyes have to do with our thought life within the intellect, the ears have to do with our emotional life within our volition.

As we can see, this symbolic alphabet is surprisingly logical and intuitive. The inner meaning of any symbol can be discerned on an intellectual level by taking five things into consideration:

1. The function of the symbol (e.g., Water is useful for cleaning. What is it that cleans our spirits? The truth about the Lord and spiritual reality in general, both of which inspire us to live a new life.)

2. The process described by the symbol (e.g., The sea churns. What of the spirit is churning and restless? Selfish desires, for example.)

3. The inherent state or quality of the symbol (e.g., A tree demonstrates beautiful order and reaches up toward the sky just as a mind structured by wisdom is beautifully ordered and attempts to reach up to know God, to catch his light.)

4. The explanation of a symbol contained within the Bible itself (e.g., The parable of the sower reveals that seeds are truths from the Word of God.)

5. The meaning of proper nouns in the original language (e.g., The name *Rachel* means "a ewe, or female sheep," so we would consider what a ewe might represent based on the above four options. Sheep are gentle and willing to follow, relying on the wisdom of the shepherd. They symbolize innocence.)

There is another tool for gaining insight into the meaning of symbols in the Word. We can enter deeply and empathically into the stories in which they appear. In many ways, I prefer this method because in addition to arriving at an intellectually neat and coherent message, we also experience a stirring of the heart. We not only see but also feel the Lord's presence in our lives. When we enter into the experiences and emotions of the Bible characters, we know what states of mind God is speaking to within the given story. This provides us with context for the other symbols that are employed. The inspiration for my previous book, *12 Miracles of Spiritual Growth,* arose out of insights gained while meditating on the emotional experiences of those people who were healed by Jesus.

In the Creation story, of course, there isn't a lot of empathizing that can occur. So in this case, we should look to interpreting its spiritual message by trying to understand it as an unfolding process of symbolism. Creation is described as occurring in seven days. A literalistic meaning requires us to believe, despite glaring scientific evidence to the contrary, that the physical earth was created in just that amount of time. A symbolic reading of that same story, on the other hand, describes how God evolves our spirit until we are finally made into his image and likeness. This symbolic interpretation offers a drastically different and, at least in my life, profoundly more useful meaning than does the literalistic interpretation.

A day is the process of darkness and cold yielding to light and warmth before fading again to darkness and cold. We recall that light symbolizes truth about spiritual matters, such as about God and about our own spiritual composition. We intuitively know that warmth symbolizes love. So day and night describe a process by which we alternate between having greater perception and having weakened perception of God's truth and love. We must experience such alternating states so that we are inspired to further our spiritual progress and to keep our arrogance at bay. Thus, the symbolism of the Creation story is internally coherent in that we know our propensity for losing track of God's love and light.

It is a deep and wonderful experience when the internal cohesion of the Bible's inner meaning is seen firsthand. The obvious, fundamental commands and literal statements revealed in the Bible serve as a compass, and the language of symbols is the path that opens up before us as we adventure into the rich landscape that surrounds our spiritual journey toward God.

Seven Days *of* Spiritual Evolution

OUR TWO BODIES

In the beginning . . . God created the heavens and the earth.

(Genesis 1:1)

In the first verse of Genesis, we read that God created the heavens and the earth. If we consider this to be a symbolic description of the very beginning of the creation of a human life, we can understand this to mean we are created such as to have two parts to our being: a spiritual part (*the heavens*), which is primary, and a natural part—that is, a part that's based in physical reality—which is represented by *the earth*. We have two bodies, an earthly body, which we are all very familiar with, and a spiritual, or heavenly, body.

This is important information. Imagine trying to get around without even being aware of the fact that you have a physical body; we wouldn't even know to *try* to get around. We can hardly navigate the realm of spirit without knowing anything about our spiritual body. The spiritual body has eyes, ears, a mouth, a nose, hands, a heart, lungs, legs, and everything else. This body is not a metaphorical body; it's real. Every faith and spiritual tradition I've ever encountered describes human beings as composed of two fundamental elements—a physical body and a spiritual body. These traditions also describe an intimate connection between the two such that the spirit is primary and causal. The spirit animates the body in much the same way that a hand animates a glove or that our body's motion animates the clothes we wear. Indeed, *anima,* the Latin root of the word *animation,* means "spirit." We can clearly see this causal relationship in specific ways. For example, emotions animate our face, thoughts animate our words, and intentions animate our behaviors. The body is the avatar of these more interior experiences.

Two valuable ideas I have received from Swedenborg are his detailed descriptions of the spiritual world (including our spiritual bodies) and of the relationship between the spiritual and natural realms. He claimed to have accurate information about the spiritual world based on extensive experiences within that realm. His descriptions are convincing, in part because they make so much sense. The fact that Swedenborg had a number of remarkable clairvoyant experiences also amplifies credence. In 1759, for example, while at a dinner party in Gothenburg, he suddenly stated that a terrible fire was raging out of control in his hometown of Stockholm, some 250 miles away. He described details of the fire as it was happening, finally stating that it was successfully extinguished a few houses away from his own. Swedenborg's statements were confirmed as true a couple days later when news of the fire finally reached Gothenburg.

Swedenborg says that through deep, prolonged meditation on the Bible, he awoke to his spiritual body so fully that he traveled through the spiritual realm, interacting with those who had passed on from this world. He states that the spiritual body is in every way the same as our physical body, but it is more essential, substantial, and perfect—that the spiritual world is profoundly more real than the physical and that the material realm is an image or reflection of the spiritual realm. Our bodies, then, reflect our spirits as a mirror reflects a living face.

The Correspondence of the Spiritual and Physical Bodies

Hidden within our everyday language are rich descriptions of the nature of our spirit. This unconscious knowledge is evidence that though we cannot overtly sense our spiritual body, its existence and nature press into and shape the way we think.

> Nothing can happen in the body unless it comes from the mind. The mind is our spirit, and the spirit is just as much a person as we are. The only difference is that the things that happen in the body happen on the physical level and the things that happen in the mind happen on the spiritual level. There is a perfect parallelism. (*Divine Providence* §296:15)

You probably know more about your spiritual body than you think. Here are some examples:

- The eyes of the spirit don't see physical light; they see truth. We use the expression *I see,* for example, to convey understanding. We also talk of *enlightenment* and *seeing the light.* Helen Keller spoke of seeing a light that was not extinguished by her physical blindness.

- If vision refers to the intellectual perception of truth, then hearing refers to *concordance,* which in the original Latin means "with-heartness." *I hear you!* means that I empathize with you or that I can relate to your emotions. Music moves our emotions and aligns them with those of the composer.

- Our spiritual sense of smell refers to our ability to instinctually perceive something as either good or bad. We get a feeling that something is off, even though we can't explain why intellectually. If something *smells fishy* or we *smell a rat,* we are referring to our perception of something being awry.

- The spirit of one person is able to touch the spirit of another, just as we can reach out with our physical hand to touch the body of another. The words *Her speech really touched me* mean that we were moved emotionally by what she said.

- We experience feelings with our spiritual skin, just as we feel objects with our physical skin. We say *He has a thin skin* to describe a person who is very sensitive and becomes upset easily.

- In the realm of spirit, our legs are our ability and our motivation to move from one state of mind to another. *A thousand-mile journey begins with a single step* is a famous saying from the *Tao Te Ching*. The legs taking that step are not physical, and the thousand-mile journey refers to progressing from one state of mind to a better state of mind.

- Just as we use our physical hands and arms to do work and achieve our earthly goals, we use our spiritual arms and hands to do our spiritual work and achieve the desires of our spirit. This power flows directly into the things we do with our physical body. In this way, our physical body is the ultimate extension of our spiritual arms, serving as the hands of the spirit and reaching into the material realm. This, Swedenborg tells us, explains why Jesus, the physical manifestation of God, is referred to as the arm of the Lord: "He saw that there was no one, and was appalled that there was no one to intervene; so his own arm brought him victory, and his righteousness upheld him" (Isaiah 59:16).

- A global symbol for love, the heart pumps blood to every single cell in our body and so sustains all; and the network of blood vessels joins all members as one, which corresponds to the expression of God's perfect love that joins all human beings and all life as one. The heart of our spirit is God's love present within us.

- We *chew things over* and *ruminate* on our experiences. Going deeper into the mind, we *digest* information to understand and make sense of our experiences. The way in which our mind incorporates information and experiences things mirrors how the intestines extract what is of value from physical food.

- Spiritual kidneys are our mind's ability to filter out toxic values and thoughts. The spiritual lungs are what allow us to breathe God's Holy Spirit into our lives and expel self-based thinking.

- Our spirit exists within a spiritual landscape, just as surely as our body exists in a physical one. We speak of *states of mind* and *psychological states,* for example, just as we use the word *state* to refer to a physical place. This use of language is mirrored in religious traditions as well. Jesus said, "The kingdom of God is among you" (Luke 17:21) and "I go and prepare a place for you" (John 14:3). In the Buddhist tradition, people speak of *reaching* nirvana, which is described in some passages as a state of mind and in others as a place. Hindu texts and mystics describe *arriving* at planes of spiritual reality.

Swedenborg's descriptions of the spiritual realm resemble accounts of near-death experiences—ineffable, living beauty that is laden with meaning beyond the surface appearances. Having had extensive spiritual experiences during the final two decades of his life, he became familiar with the laws that govern the spiritual realm, one of which is that distance in the spiritual world is determined according to states of mind. People who are in similar states of mind will find themselves in close proximity to each other and within similar landscapes— landscapes that are symbolic representations of those very states of mind. And to the extent that two people are in dissimilar states of mind, they will be distant from one another.

This fact, according to Swedenborg, explains why there is a heaven and a hell and why they are separate from each other. People whose minds are governed by love are in heaven, while those who pursue only self-interests and disregard the well-being of others are in hell. It would be more accurate to say they *are heaven* or *are hell* rather than to say they are *in heaven* or *in hell*, because state of mind both *determines* and *creates* place. Surroundings in the spiritual world are manifestations of state of mind. We sometimes experience this when dreaming. For example, when we fall asleep in a tense mood, we may experience a tense situation in an unpleasant environment. On the other hand, when we have a beautiful dream, we may awake in a state of peace or joy.

Hell isn't a punishment; it's a selfish state of mind and the spiritual surroundings that are created by that state of mind. The lakes of unquenchable fire mentioned in the book of Revelation are the external manifestations of burning lusts for power, money, pleasure, and so on—things that cannot be satiated and so are inherently torturous. The *outer darkness* mentioned by Jesus in the Gospels expresses a state of mind that is profoundly blind to spiritual truths. Again, it is not a punishment but is the natural consequence of self-focused living and thinking. So, in the spiritual realm, state of mind determines place and landscape.

Spirit Precedes Matter

In the first sentence of Genesis, the word *heavens* precedes the word *earth*, revealing the idea that the realm of spirit is causal to the material realm in a way similar to how our thoughts cause our movements. Since spirit precedes matter in this manner, our bodies in the material realm can be seen to house and give expression to the spiritual qualities discussed above. Our spiritual body is more substantial and real than our material body, because it interacts with that which is more real than the fleeting things of the temporal realm.

> I can assert that those things that are in the spiritual world are more real than those in the natural world, for the dead part that is added in nature to the spiritual does not constitute reality but diminishes it. This is evident from the state of the angels of heaven compared with the state of men on the earth, and from all things that are in heaven compared with all things in the world. (*Apocalypse Explained* §1218:3)

It interacts with *ideals,* in the Platonic sense of the word—eternal, nonphysical realities from which earthly reality takes form. Because the spiritual body is outside of the realm of space, it is not bound by its laws; and because the spiritual body is outside the realm of time, it is eternal. The parallel between the physical and spiritual bodies is not a clever play on words or merely symbolic; it is a fundamental reality characterized by a causal relationship that we typically view in reverse order, the cookie looking at the cookie cutter.

We may wonder why God does not create us as spiritual beings who would not have to endure the pain, confusion, and limitations of life in the material realm. Limitations are our ultimate blessings. The world of spirit is perfect. If such a world was all we ever knew, we would see truth perfectly and our hearts would be perfectly aligned with God's will. And this would be true for everyone. Thus, there would be no discrepancies in perception, thought, or will between us and any other being. Indeed, without any distinctions, there would only be one being. We would have no individuation and so no relationship; love requires individuation and relationship. We must have limitations, each one unique and formed by the crucible of space and time, to give us our own view on life and God and to make unique our way of receiving and giving love. These limitations that make us who we are therefore allow us to have a relationship with other people and with God. We learn from others. We learn to love others and ourselves despite our limitations and the selfishness caused by those limitations. Loving only perfection isn't love. For God's selfless, eternal love to be real, it must be manifested and perceived. Thus, divine love exists for the sake of its realization, and its realization can occur only within the limitations of space and time—the material realm. Life on earth provides us with the most precious yet devastating gift of divine love—sense of selfhood. Much of what will be discussed in the rest of this book has to do with what I consider to be this most holy and most dangerous gift.

We may also wonder why we have a spiritual body. The same space-time that gives rise to the material body also destroys the material body. When viewed from the eternal realm, the merely temporal expression and perception of love can be said to have never even existed. This is why we must have two bodies. The love we experience while on earth is actually experienced by the spiritual body through the physical body, as has been described above. Every time we feel love for another, for God, for goodness, or for truth, and every time we feel empathy, we are doing so from within the spiritual body by means of the physical body. Since love, truth, empathy, wisdom, and the like are of the spiritual realm, they are eternal and remain as part of the eternal spirit. Experiences of love and insight are stored up within so that when the material body falls away, we awaken in fullness to the spiritual body that has developed unbeknownst to us while we were still on earth. On earth, this body seems only an ethereal thing. But because all our experiences of love and insight have occurred through the sense of selfhood arising from the physical body, this sense of selfhood and all it carries is imprinted upon the spirit. And what remains is our sense of individuation based in the unique states of love and spiritual insight that we experienced in our limited state on earth. Since we can as individuated spirits interact with one another and continue to be in relationship with God, we can continue to grow and evolve even after death.

Jesus says, "The last will be first, and the first will be last" (Matthew 20:16). Some people are born into loving homes, loving communities, and stable genetics. Others are not as fortunate. It can be much more difficult to access and express love when we have not often received it, when we have not been educated in love, or when our genetics inhibit us in some way. Imagine when such an individual awakens after death to the unstoppable, infinite love of God; he or she will know the value of this love in a way not known to others. We are given to continue in our relationship with God and others even after the death of the material body; we will forever learn truth and grow ever wiser.

In the pages that follow, we will take a walk together to see how our mind can evolve from selfishness arising from a state of dark delusion (**Day 0**)—the delusion that selfhood is real—to a state of love based in the spiritual light that reveals sense of selfhood to be a functional illusion. We do not actually *have* life but instead are *recipients of* life.

SUGGESTED PRACTICES

Reflecting on this chapter's discussion of having two bodies—a *spiritual*, or *heavenly*, body and a *physical*, or *earthly*, body—your practice will focus on learning to become aware of and to appreciate both of these glorious gifts. This can be done in the midst of normal daily activities as well as during focused regular meditative practices.

Cultivating Awareness in Daily Activities

As you move through your day, marvel at your wondrous physical body. It is an amazing servant, gentle and compliant.

You may even want to take some time out to appreciate and be grateful for your body, experiencing the different sensations that come along with each of its parts. Many people experience chronic pain, suffer from a disability, have a health issue, or are dissatisfied with the shape of their body. Any of these things can make it difficult to appreciate the body. If this is the case for you, remember that God's life breathes into all living creatures just the same. Regardless of our particular physical impairments, we all struggle on as best we can no matter how difficult our situation. While our bodies are imperfect, they are still amazing and deserving of love. As we are told that we are made in the image and likeness of God, certainly God loves the physical body that allows our spirits to express themselves.

When you can begin to appreciate your physical body, you should then move inward and try to catch your spiritual body in action. Recall the different functions of mind and heart that are indeed the spiritual body's activity—using your spiritual legs to move away from a negative state toward a more positive one; using your spiritual vision to gain insight; using your spiritual digestive tract to transform experiences into meaningful, productive thoughts and motivations; etc.

Meditative Practice

It is valuable to have a process, an induction, by which to transition from normal consciousness, which is characterized by beta brain waves, to a meditative state, which is characterized by slower brain waves. The following induction serves the goal of meditation in several ways: 1) It gathers attention away from normal daily thought patterns and focuses the mind inward. 2) It is designed to be relaxing to both body and mind. 3) It brings a sense of oneness within awareness. 4) Finally, after repeating an induction prior to each one of multiple meditation sessions, the induction can catalyze more rapid entry into a meditative state of mind. The mind comes to know the induction as an invitation to meditate, and it will respond to that invitation accordingly. This induction is intended to introduce the meditation for this chapter, which begins on the next page, and the meditation for the **Day 0** chapter (p. 37, below).

Meditation Induction 1

Get into a comfortable, seated position so that you are relaxed but won't fall asleep. You may wish to sit in the lotus, half-lotus, or cross-legged position. If you are unable to get into any of these positions or simply prefer sitting regularly, please sit in a chair, with your back straight, your hands either resting on your thighs or folded in your lap, and your feet flat on the floor.

Focusing on the sensation of the breath in your nose, breathe in slowly and deeply, sensing also the expansion of your belly as it fills with air and then holding it for the count of three, two, and one. Now . . . release the breath slowly.

Again, focusing on the sensation of the breath in your nose, breathe in slowly and deeply, noticing your belly as it rises and then holding it for the count of five, four, three, two, and one. Exhale slowly.

One more time, focusing on the sensation of the breath in your nose, breathe in slowly and deeply, being aware of its intimate relationship with your belly and then holding it for the count of seven, six, five, four, three, two, and one. Breathe out slowly.

In the quiet that follows, breathing normally, focus on the sensation of the breath flowing in and out of your nose.

[Pause for 2 minutes; then begin the appropriate chapter's meditation]

Meditation—Our Two Bodies

From within this meditative state, lovingly scan your body with your mind. As though your mind moves like water, start at the top of your head and flow down through your face and skull to your torso and arms, washing downward into your legs and then out through your feet. With a deep sense of gratitude for each part of your body, move your awareness upward from your feet but this time more slowly, taking time to thank each part of your body for the service it provides.

[Pause slightly after each of the following body parts, pausing a little longer after moving past the pelvic region]

Your feet; your ankles; your lower legs; your knees; your thighs; your pelvic region; your abdomen; your hands; your fingers; your lower arms; your elbows; your upper arms; your chest cavity; your heart and lungs; your back; your shoulders; your neck; your throat in front and then spine in back, curving gracefully up to the base of your skull; the back of your head; your ears; your jaw; your mouth and tongue and teeth; your lips; your cheeks; your nose; your eyes; your forehead; and finally, the top of your head.

Your body is a magnificent gift from God. It is a selfless servant. Inhale deeply and slowly. Hold it.

[Pause for a couple seconds]

Now, release the breath.

[Pause for a few seconds]

Breathe in and out in this way a few more times. With each breath in, think to yourself, "Thank you, Lord." And with each breath out, mentally repeat, "for my body." Our body functions as the blessed instrument of our spirit, so spend a few moments appreciating your physical body in this way.

[Pause for 1 minute]

Just as we have a physical body, we also have a spiritual body; and each of our two bodies can be appreciated for the gift that it is. Now, listen to and mentally join in the following prayer:

Lord, thank you for our spiritual vision.

We thank you for the ability to understand spiritual ideas, the truth about who you are, and the truth about who we are.

Thank you for our spiritual hearing.

We thank you for the ability to relate to people on an emotional level—to resonate with them, to hear where they are coming from, and to empathize with them.

Thank you for our spiritual sense of smell.

We thank you for the ability to sense if a situation, idea, or choice we make is good or bad.

Thank you for our spiritual arms.

We thank you for the ability to touch the lives of other people for the sake of goodness—to be strong in our service to you and your purposes.

Thank you for our spiritual legs.

We thank you for the freedom to be who we want to be— to choose our own path.

Thank you for our spiritual digestive tract.

We thank you for the ability to understand our day-to-day experiences, throwing out what is worthless and incorporating what is valuable.

Thank you for our spiritual skeleton.

We thank you for the sense of self that gives shape to who we are in this world.

Thank you for our spiritual lungs, our spiritual breathing.

We thank you for the ability to communicate with those

things that are higher than the things of the earth, to receive inflow from the spiritual world, and to gain wisdom that will help guide our perspective and emotions.

Thank you for our spiritual heart.

We thank you for the capacity to feel passionate about life, to pursue what is good, to feel love for others, and to feel adoration and gratitude toward you. We thank you for your love, the life force that animates our entire being.

In the quiet that follows, allow God's love to wash over you so that you may enter deeply into faith and be present in the light of spirit.

Doing Practice

Intentionally perform an action of love while at the same time knowing that any action of love could not possibly arise from the illusion of selfhood; it arises from God's love alone. Now you are breathing with your spiritual body. You are breathing in the truth that all love is of God and breathing out the false idea that we can love of ourselves.

Suggested Questions for Pondering and/or Discussion

- What did you experience while sensing your physical body? Were you able to be grateful and rejoice in your body? Did you notice any connection between state of mind (spirit) and the body?

- What did it mean to catch your spiritual body in action? Were you moved by the emotions of another person? What did you hear with your spirit? How did you use your spiritual eyes? How are you using your spiritual arms to touch others? With your spiritual legs, were you able to walk away from negative thinking or destructive desires toward a better place? Is your spiritual heart healthy and able to love others without judgment? Did you have any spiritual insights?

- During the meditation, what was it like to give thanks to the parts of your spiritual body? Did you experience them in a way that was different from how you experienced them during your daily activities? If so, how?

- How did it feel to intentionally perform an act of love while knowing that it arises from God's love?

- Do you have any further reflections concerning this chapter?

DAY 0: WHERE WE BEGIN

The earth was a formless void and darkness
covered the face of the deep.

(Genesis 1:2)

It would have been helpful to know where I began that Sunday walk in San Francisco; it is even more important to know where we begin the journey that is life. This second verse of Genesis is a symbolic description of where we all begin. If having information about where we begin is the good news, the bad news is the content of that information: that we are born into spiritual darkness, void of any genuine love.

The idea that we are born without any spiritual goodness is a controversial idea, commonly accepted among most Christian denominations but rejected by other belief systems. Hinduism, for example, claims that our atman, or spirit, is divine. Humanism espouses the idea that humans are inherently good, attributing the failure of this goodness to express itself to environmental factors. At the heart of this controversy is the question of who we are: what is the nature of self?

When at Grinnell College, I took a class on the religious philosophies of the world. Our beloved teacher, Dr. Burkle, held that thinkers tend to fall into two basic camps: unifiers, who see commonalities and bridges between ideas and traditions, and dividers, who focus on differences. As one who tends toward unification, I don't see any contradictions between these varied ideas on the nature of the self. Before exploring this, though, it is valuable to clarify the nature of spiritual, or selfless, love. I will refer to this love as *genuine love.*

When we love others not for what they do for us or even mean to us on a personal level, but rather because we believe in the value of love as something greater than our personal needs and wants, we are entering into a love that transcends our personhood. It does so in two ways. First, when we enter genuine love, as just mentioned, we become *a part of something greater than ourselves.* The self is subsumed into the whole, to which it is now in service. This greater whole may be as large as communion with all humanity or as small as the relationship between two people.

Second, genuine love is *unity itself.* The selfless love each and every one of us feels and lives out is the same selfless love. If it was *my* selfless love or *her* selfless love, it would still be of the self and so not actually selfless. I like to think of genuine love as the blood in our body—the individual arteries and capillaries deliver the blood to different areas, but the blood itself is not changed in any way by having passed through a particular vessel. Though each of us is distinct, like the individual capillaries, the genuine love that flows through our lives is singular; it is oneness.

This selfless love is that which drives the evolutionary pattern of unification, as we will discuss at the end of this book. Not only, therefore, do we enter into a community that is greater than our individual selves, but we also experience the oneness of love itself—an essence that is greater than any being who experiences it or lives it out.

From here, it isn't much of a leap to say that God's fundamental nature is selfless love and that any genuine love we experience is only ever *of* God. I therefore agree with the Christian view that selfhood is darkness and in and of itself void of spiritual goodness, just like a capillary in and of itself is an empty vessel. We can be rescued from that darkness only through God's selfless love, which is effectively more real than ourselves and not something we produce ourselves. We might describe this initial state of darkness, which is void of any genuine love, as **Day 0**—the day before God shines his light upon us.

When genuine love comes to live within us and motivate us, it is God's living spirit moving us from within as if it were our own spirit. If being part of the joy and unity of genuine love is the purpose for which we have been created and we all begin at **Day 0,** it must be that human nature is designed to *evolve* toward genuine love. Such a design conforms to those worldviews that propose innate goodness.

Carl Rogers (1902–87), a pioneer in the field of psychology, was a primary proponent of humanism in the twentieth century. He believed we all have an innate but often stymied drive toward self-realization; in other words, it is in our nature to evolve into our highest, most wise, most productive, and most peaceful possible state. If we accept that this drive to evolve spiritually is of God, then there is no contradiction between admitting the self to be completely void of spiritual goodness and acknowledging that God is constantly working from within to evolve us through mechanisms of which we usually know nothing whatsoever. I have come to believe that there is no actual selfhood. The spiritual darkness, which is void of love, is the result of our delusional faith in the self as something real, when in fact the self is not real. This will be discussed further throughout the book.

The fact that human beings are the most recent and wondrous step in the evolving universe suggests to me that we can find a more complete and unified vision of the Divine within ourselves than within other entities of the natural world (it is crucial, though, to see that our existence is interdependent with all of creation). We are the beings most analogous to God, since we are made in his image, as we will explore further in **Day 6.** We are human because God is human. He is the divine human. What is truly human, therefore, is of God. This means that genuine love is truly human, and it is the force that drives the ever-evolving perfection of the universe. So I agree with Rogers when he says that what makes us human is what moves us toward fulfilling and actualizing our greatest potential, toward what is good. God's spirit evolves us from within. Swedenborg writes:

> Here is how matters stand with all the different types of goodness that make up heavenly life (and therefore eternal life) in a person or an angel: At the core of anything good is the Lord himself and consequently goodness grounded in love, which comes directly from him. . . . The pattern actually ordained for humans, then, is to live a life of goodness received from the Lord, that is, to live a life inspired by the Lord. This influence is constant and involves itself in each and every effort of our will, guiding it as much as possible in the direction of the ordained plan. Our own will, of course, is constantly leading us the opposite direction. (*Secrets of Heaven* §9683:1, 2)

Since the Divine alone is genuine love and so alone is actually human, the Divine alone is able to spiritually evolve us. On a spiritual level, then, there is no actual self. Many mystics, both Western and Eastern, have sustained this idea that there is no actual selfhood, or that self is empty. Selfhood is a sense of separation arising from the fact that our consciousness is bound in space and time. One of the benefits of withdrawing and quieting the mind through meditation is a weakening of the delusion of selfhood and consequent awakening to our unity with all other beings in God.

What I am driving at is that all good is only ever of God and that where there is an absence of goodwill and kindness, there is a distortion and partial absence of God. What we think of as self is the product of the boundaries limiting God's expression within us. Just as an absence of light creates a shadow but that shadow is not an actual thing, the absence of God is what creates our sense of individuality, or self, which also is not an actual thing.

The void described in Genesis 1:2 symbolizes the total absence of genuine love when we have faith in self and not in God. Jesus speaks of this kind of love when he urges us to love our enemies, to do good to those who spitefully use us, to turn the other cheek, and to lay down our lives—our selfhood—for the sake of blessing others. This kind of loving service to even those who harm us is diametrically opposed to how we instinctually feel when faced with a spiteful person. In the absence of God, we are completely void of genuine love. Before God sheds spiritual light upon our lives, we are completely in the dark. It is not possible for us to start in any worse a place. But while being born void of genuine love and in utter darkness seems like bad news, it is actually wonderful news. As we begin our walk through Genesis 1, a recurring theme is that what seems to be bad is in fact beneficial. Starting out completely in utter ignorance and depravity means that we have everything to gain. We do not arrive at God's perfection but instead evolve and grow forever. That's very good news. Imagine an eternity of having arrived—it couldn't get more boring than that. There would be nothing new to learn, no more progress or personal development, and no new depths of love to experience.

Being infinite, or beyond anything that heaven or earth can embody, God's love cannot be communicated in a state of stasis but only by the processes of material and spiritual evolution. Because there is no ratio between space-time and the infinite and eternal God, this evolving communication can never reach completion. What this means is that we are in a sense already in heaven. The progression itself is inherently good, and so the moments that make up that progression are in service to it, even when they are of themselves hellish. The end is good and everything exists and progresses toward that end. I believe one of the reasons we are born into utter darkness is so that we can enjoy the never-ending experience of increasing love. For light to illuminate, there must be darkness. Though this darkness allows for human evil, true selfless love uses evil situations to reveal itself and evolve us and so triumphs. For example, peace rallies and movements are born out of widespread hatred and violence.

Earth is exciting and so potently mesmerizing—the lights, colors, sounds, smells, tastes, and touches can be enthralling. Because the things of spirit are much more hidden and subtle, it is easy for us to become so absorbed in the material realm that we fail to even realize there is a spiritual realm at all. Without making focused, conscious efforts to awaken and remain awake to the life of the spirit through praying, meditating, and reading spiritual texts, worldly concerns consume the mind. Even with concerted effort, the things of the world easily control us.

Our spiritual understanding need not always come about by means of formal learning. Being loved initiates us into the life of love. Being forgiven can inspire us to forgive. I have met many wonderful non-religious people; and I have asked a number of them how they are able to sustain kindness without making a conscious effort to be connected with God.

One young woman who stayed as a volunteer at our children's home in Nepal stated that she was raised by parents who refused to ever speak negatively about anyone. She said it had made a lasting impression on her and that she chose to live her life in the same way. Her friend, who also volunteered with us, provided an almost opposite explanation. She had grown up in a family torn apart by conflict, where she had felt largely unloved. The wounds she endured inspired her to never inflict such pain on others, and she was determined to be as loving a person as she could be. While neither of these women indicated that they were making conscious efforts toward God, their stories reveal that they are indeed aspiring to something higher than their selfhood. They are aspiring to genuine love, which is God. A life of love, not mere verbal expression of faith, is the true worship of God. Whether we are introduced to spiritual ideals through formal education or through life experiences, to sustain a higher spiritual state of mind requires effort. Intentional devotion to God conditions us to be better recipients of genuine love.

Our Default State of Mind

The formless void of darkness in which we start our spiritual lives is the default state of mind that focuses on the things of the earth. The term *formless* used in Genesis 1:2 symbolizes that human consciousness during **Day 0** is absent of spiritual knowledge and consequently without form of thought. Our mind, therefore, is *formless* before we apprehend and find value in spiritual concepts, such as clemency and restraint. Just as knowledge of math, grammar, physics, music, and the like structure our external thinking, spiritual values, ideals, truth about God, and truth about the nature of the human spirit structure spiritual minds that reach up beyond the material world. Until the ideal of forgiveness sinks into our minds and hearts, our instinct is to hold a grudge. Before we decide to employ our energies for the betterment of society, for example, our default position is to use our energies to better our own position within society. This is not to say it is all or nothing; our minds can possess spiritual structure at a variety of stages and be spiritually motivated in varying degrees. We are spiritually formless, though, to the extent that we are without the mental structures necessary to lift us up above self-based thoughts.

Without any spiritual concepts to lift our mind out of default self-absorption, we cannot experience the joy of spiritual love. As mentioned above, self cannot offer self*less* love. And since self cannot even really struggle with itself, neither can it transcend itself. Only to the extent that we see through the delusion of self as the source of its own life, its own thoughts, and its own love are we capable of spiritual love. Until then, we are void of real love. It is important to remember that people who live a life of selfless love are on some level seeing through the delusion of self, even if not on a conscious, intentional level.

Void is used here to describe a mind without love. At the end of this book, we will look at how the evolving natural universe is an ever-opening revelation of divine love and how we can therefore understand the fundamental essence of reality—the I AM—as divine love. Love is spiritual substance; it is the essential nature of God and so of reality. Love is the only real thing. *Void* means "an absence of substance"; thus, a spiritual void is an absence of love. If *formless* refers to an absence of spiritual understanding about love, *void* refers to a lack of genuine love itself.

Clearly, this is a very dark state of mind. Before our consciousness begins to evolve with both ideals of love and the *desire* to love, we are spiritually blind and in the dark. So complete is our blindness that we don't even know that we are blind or that there is such a thing as light. We are suffering a delusion within a delusion, which is what is meant by *the earth was a formless void and darkness covered the face of the deep.* Our ignorance of our own delusion of selfhood is the *darkness* that enwraps *the face of the deep.* When we are trapped in this double delusion, there's no way we can escape it on our own. We need spiritual light to wake us up to the fact that we are deluded. We need divine intervention. Fortunately, being divine love, God adores us and is waiting to lift us out of the darkness. As we will see in **Day 1,** he hovers over us, waiting to shine the truth of his love into our lives.

Just as important as knowing that we begin our journey in a place that is void of spirit is knowing God's infinite love for us. In fact, the two go hand in hand: knowing God's love requires knowing our complete lack of love; knowing God's mercy requires recognizing our utter need for mercy; knowing God's wisdom depends on how well we know our total absence of wisdom. Without knowing darkness, we cannot recognize light; without sensing spiritual meaninglessness, we cannot know the value of meaning. Our hindrances are also our blessings. Conversely, experiencing God's love reveals how loveless we are, and seeing God's wisdom reveals our ignorance. For example, simply noticing the elegant order and beauty of a leaf can move us to awe and make us realize that we are nothing in comparison to the Creator. God's glory shows us our dross.

In a life focused only on self and the things of the world, we will miss out on the sweetness and happiness of love. Selfish pursuits inherently lead to unhappiness and frustration for a number of reasons. First, they are constrained by the laws of the natural world. Coveting what we can't have leads to misery. Love, however, is not bound. We can love others at any time and at any place, even if it is by praying for them or fostering goodwill toward them.

Second, self-oriented pleasures are always fleeting. No amount of alcohol is enough for those who seek happiness in the bottle. No amount of pleasure is enough for those who seek happiness in sensuality. No amount of money, food, or power is sufficient to satiate those desires. These are the flames of hell, which are described in the Bible as unquenchable. What could be more hellish than an unquenchable appetite?

Third, there is no freedom in the pursuit of worldly pleasures. We are actually slaves, driven robotically by these insatiable drives. When we function by and for the physical level of our being, we operate within the mechanical cause-and-effect rules of space-time. We are essentially a cog in a machine, void of life.

This is what I understand when Jesus says, "Everyone who commits sin is a slave to sin" (John 8:34). Immediately before this statement, he says, "If you continue in my word, you are truly my disciples; and you will know the truth, and the truth will make you free" (John 8:31–32). Since love transcends space-time, awakening to genuine love is to live and be free for the first time. Jesus's words, if we are willing to follow and continue in them, lead to a liberating truth: the core of his message is that we love. Spiritual truth structures our mind to allow for love and for freedom from the mechanical existence of living from and for the delusion of selfhood and its desires. When we choose to love and feel the joy inherent within love, we are free.

The inherent misery within the void and darkness of selfishness eventually causes us to seek light. Being born in a state of total spiritual ignorance, we can only ever *grow* in wisdom; and there is no end to that wisdom. Just as the universe is perpetually evolving, so does our mind perpetually evolve in its ability to receive and communicate spiritual wisdom and genuine love. It is vital to know that when we begin our journey, we are completely formless and enwrapped in darkness; it is equally important to know that we are also infinitely loved by God.

When we begin to progress to higher states of consciousness founded on love and structured by spiritual truth, it would be a mistake to think we have left the darkness behind. We read later, at **Day 4,** that God calls the darkness *night* and sets it in opposition to *day;* and he says that the motions of the sun and moon, which relate to day and night, are for our seasons and division of time. This shows that there is value in the darkness. Even at **Day 6,** darkness is still playing its important role: "And there was evening and there was morning, the sixth day" (Genesis 1:31).

The persistence of darkness is a blessing in disguise. We never want to forget that a part of us is perpetually prone to selfishness and to succumbing to the delusions that support that selfishness. Part of the thick darkness in which we begin is a kind of self-reliant arrogance. Understanding our inherent and perpetual darkness allows us to remain humble and thus in the light. Such humility leads us to daily seek God's help, knowing that on our own, we would sink back into the darkness. Awareness of the darkness also imbues us with empathy. We know what it's like to be enslaved within the delusion of self, so we are then empowered to forgive and love others despite their shortcomings.

Our spiritual evolution is not a perfectly uniform progression. We evolve in circles and cycles, in waves and tides. We may make important strides against a harmful habit only to slip back for some time before regaining our ground, but we gain something very important through this varied evolutionary process: humility. We can observe how different aspects of our being evolve at different rates and begin at different times. We may understand the idea of laying down our lives for others when it comes to helping the needy, for example, but not the idea of laying down our judgments against our family and friends. We may quickly recognize and overcome a habit of backbiting, but only later do we recognize and begin to refrain from a more subtle habit, such as omitting the truth.

Our underlying state of darkness also serves us well as a counterpoint and contrast to our better states. Harking back to a previous idea, it is progression and not some static state that best expresses love. Feeling less loving for a while reminds us of how good it is to be in more loving states. When we get used to the good states in our everyday lives, we begin to take them for granted and no longer value or even perceive them. After an hour in a room filled with roses, we'll no longer notice the fragrance. If we eat only our one favorite food on a daily basis, we'll learn to loathe it. If we experience only a blank white wall without any shades of color, our vision will fade. When two people deeply love each other, a time of disagreement and frustration leads in the end to increased gratitude for the other. The unhappiness of the cold accentuates the value of the relationship itself and of the other person. We need contrast in spiritual things, just as we do in these worldly things. So retaining some times of darkness in our lives is necessary for the continuing evolution of love occurring within us.

We can see this dialectic displayed in the symbiotic relationships of nature. The microbes, plants, birds, crocodiles, and fish from earlier stages of natural evolution serve as foundations for later manifestations of evolution, such as complex mammals. No mammal could survive without microbes and plants. The extinction of lower life forms disrupts the entire ecosystem and causes harm to higher life forms. Indeed, it makes less sense to think of each species independently than it does to focus on the ecosystem as the primary living entity. So in our spiritual lives, each state and element of our mind has its purpose and place. Instinctual drives for physical pleasure, such as for sex and food; for dominance; and for self-preservation are all self-serving when isolated from any spiritual or social context and therefore are of themselves spiritually void. Yet each of these instincts has value when submitted to the goal of genuine love. Love, in fact, gains meaning because of a persistent backdrop of selfishness, as love that pushes through the challenges of selfish desire is proven to be genuine. Dark states, then, are elements in the symbiotic relationships that make up our spiritual evolution toward love.

There is still another way in which we can understand how the darkness has value. Our sense of self as the doer within our own self-improvement and spiritual progress is an illusion. If we believe in the sensation of selfhood as doer, we are deluded. Since it is impossible for self to transcend self, as we have seen, we can know that we are raised up above our state of darkness by God's spirit of love. This can only be effected, however, through our sense of self and our activities based in that sense of self. So we need this sense of personal volition for our spiritual evolution to be at all meaningful. According to Swedenborg:

> All freedom is a function of love and affection, because what we love we do with a sense of freedom. . . .
>
> The Lord leads us toward goodness by means of our freedom: he uses our freedom to deflect us from evil and bend us toward goodness, leading us so gently and subtly that we believe the whole process is coming from ourselves. . . .
>
> We need to compel ourselves not to do evil . . . and also compel ourselves to do good, doing so as though we were doing it on our own, but acknowledging that goodness comes from the Lord. (*New Jerusalem* §148:1, 3, 4)

We need our sense of selfhood to give and receive love on a more fundamental level. Without this sense, what is it of us that would participate in the giving and receiving of love? Love is meaningful only in the context of relationship. The darkness of the illusion of selfhood *must* remain if we are to be alive at all.

In the natural universe, I see the same message that I understand in Genesis 1:2: that starting at the lowest possible state—the formless, dark, void—is what is required for the reification of divine love. The universe began as formless, dark, and void so that it could evolve ever upward toward order, meaning, and representation of God. The same is true of our spirits. In myriads of ways, nature expresses the progression from void and darkness to what is alive and full of light; and she also reveals the value of darkness, death, and difficulty in that these things provide for new life. Nature reveals the value of what is not alive through its service to what *is* alive. The detritus of one year of life enriches the soil for a new year of life. Wide-reaching extinction events throughout Earth's biological history have invariably led to an evolutionary explosion of enriched biodiversity comprised of even more complex and beautiful organisms. A seed is locked inside a shell that is in itself dead, revealing no sign of the beauty, complexity, and usefulness that lie within. But when touched by light and water, the shell opens and the seed unfolds in a slow progression, until finally becoming a mighty tree or a beautiful flower. As these examples demonstrate, the service of lifelessness requires time to show itself.

Similarly, the lifelessness of the illusion of self serves as the seedbed for the tree of life to take root and blossom in our lives. We must have a sense of self, in order for us to experience love and its joy. The dark void of delusion serves as the cold night that gives all the more meaning to the dawn of God's light into our lives. It provides the necessary contrast from which we can begin to evolve eternally toward an image and likeness of God. So if you feel depressed about your faults, know that with your participation, they can and will eventually be made to serve a good purpose. You are on the road and that's good enough.

Just as the universe is a constantly progressing miracle that sings out incredible wisdom and all-encompassing love, so is human spiritual life. Divine love draws us ever up out of selfishness into more abundant and beautiful life. Our thoughts become ordered by divine wisdom, just as there is ever-increasing order in the natural universe. It is impossible for God's infinite love to be fully and immediately expressed within the confines of space and time, so it must express itself progressively in order to increasingly embody itself in our finite existences.

Genuine love is proven in its ability to love even when another is behaving selfishly. As Jesus states, "If you love those who love you, what credit is that to you? For even sinners love those who love them. If you do good to those who do good to you, what credit is that to you? For even sinners do the same" (Luke 6:32–33).

So far, we have looked at why we are born into the dark void and how to embrace this fact. We can gain just as much when we relate this truth to those around us. When loved ones exhibit selfishness—crossness, worldliness, vengefulness, greed, and all the rest—we should remember that none of us has been created to be perfect and that we are all in the slow and constant process of evolution, with all its seasons. If a personal relationship seems hopeless, take heart; with engaged effort, chances are that it, too, will evolve.

Broadening outward to a social view, the message contained in this seemingly simple verse can profoundly change our perspective on human society. While the daily news can fill us with horror and despair, we must remember that even though we began in the darkest place possible, we are a work in progress. Since each individual creating our global society begins in the same dark void of selfishness, it is amazing that there is any progression at all. And yet there is a great deal of progress! Fewer people than ever before are living in abject poverty; child labor is decreasing; equality between the sexes is improving; the childhood death rate is declining; literacy and level of education are rising; homicide is on the decline; and global peace is increasing. Just as the physical universe and the individual spirit evolve, so does our global society. The universe, the individual, and society all begin in darkness and without form, the conditions from which evolution is born.

SUGGESTED PRACTICES

The focus of this chapter is on recognizing that we begin life in a state of spiritual void and darkness, and understanding that this is in fact a good place to begin. The following activities and practices are designed to help bring these ideas to life.

Cultivating Awareness in Daily Activities

1

Make efforts to notice your mind as you go through your day. Recognize those feelings, thoughts, or behaviors that suggest how you are caught within the void that is the delusion of selfhood, and accept that selfishness is universally part of the process of spiritual evolution. When you notice some form of selfishness, you may want to repeat a phrase to yourself such as, "Thank you, God, for allowing me to see my shortcoming. Thank you for using it as an opportunity to grow." Remember that the mere act of noticing those moments of selfishness lets light penetrate and dispel its thick darkness. To observe and come to really know that we are by nature spiritually void is the first step toward liberation. Within lifelessness, the Lord instills life.

2

Take a walk in nature and notice all the ways in which it reflects the truth that by God's grace and mercy life miraculously arises from what is lifeless.

Meditative Practice

In the following meditation, you will be invited to observe your thoughts while remaining detached from them. Consider your thoughts to be waves on the surface of the sea. Neither resist nor pursue any of these thoughts; instead, simply observe them.

Most of our thoughts are bound to sense of self. Until we recognize this and find that place where we can detach from our thoughts, we will most likely remain bound within the delusion of self. Meditation helps separate our consciousness from this delusion of self. In very deep meditation, it is possible to enter a state of mind that is distant enough from sense of self that it moves beyond observing our self-based thoughts into having a sense of unity with all and a dissipation of sense of self. Most of the time, however, even while practicing meditation, self-based thoughts remain present. In order to recognize self-based thoughts as they arise, it is helpful to be familiar with the most common categories into which they fall. These categories include thoughts associated with:

Fear-mongering

- Worries about the future and obsessive or needless planning
- Thoughts about reputation and about what others think about us
- Thoughts about money problems
- Thoughts about status
- Health worries

Hostility

- Thoughts about perceived offenses against the self
- Thoughts about revenge
- Hopes for negative outcomes either for others or for ourselves
- Self-hatred
- Anger about life circumstances or life in general
- Anger toward God

Self-glorification

- The need to be perfect
- The need to be better than others
- Frustration about imperfections or inadequacies
- Self-justification
- Bragging
- Thoughts about how one is superior or inferior to others
- Self-judgment, judgments against others, or judgments against God

Desire

- For food
- For sexual pleasure
- For adoration or fame
- For wealth
- For specific objects (car, house, etc.)
- For drugs and/or alcohol
- For heightened spiritual or emotional experiences

Notice how all of our self-based thoughts involve deception or a lie of some kind: when we seek to gain approval or adoration, we plan what we will say, omitting certain truths and amplifying others; the belief that we are entitled to judge ourselves or others is false; we justify our actions by skewing truth; the belief that we *need* to worry is never true. These are just a few examples of the subtle lies that accompany egoic thinking.

That nearly all our thoughts are tied to the illusion of self is inevitable. This meditation is not intended as a way to judge self-based thoughts as unacceptable and make attempts at getting rid of them; rather, it is a way to simply notice, without attachment, the thoughts that arise and then to recognize and acknowledge that they arise from the illusion of self. Wonderfully, in so doing, we are propelled from the darkness of **Day 0** into the light of **Day 1**—we are seeing the truth about selfhood. Let's begin with the induction.

[Perform Meditation Induction 1 (p. 13, above)]

Meditation—**Day 0:** Where We Begin

From within this meditative state, allow yourself to notice the thoughts flowing through your mind, one leading to another . . . to another . . . to another, like waves on the sea. Imagine yourself hovering above the surface of the waters—detached, unaffected, and observant. Do not make any effort to either resist or follow a particular thought. Just let them flow.

Now, try to see how the thoughts are created by the sense of self and how they are designed to serve that sense of self.

[Pause for 10 seconds]

Do you notice any thoughts that arise from selfless love?

[Pause for 10 seconds]

In the quiet that follows, simply regard the flow of thoughts and observe their deeper source and purpose.

Doing Practice

When you encounter people behaving in ways that seem to arise from their delusion of selfhood, remember that we all not only start in this place of darkness but that this part of our being—the urge toward selfishness—remains with us forever. Know that the Lord evolves each of us according to his perfect, eternal plan—a plan that we are often not able to see. Keeping these things in mind, work at being tolerant, patient, and loving toward those who behave in self-serving ways. Try to lovingly respond to or interact with such individuals so as to perhaps help alleviate both your suffering and their own.

Suggested Questions for Pondering and/or Discussion

- What do you think of the idea that selfhood is a functional illusion? How does this idea make you feel?

- What was it like trying to notice the darker areas of your life? Did you notice any feelings, thoughts, or behaviors that showed you your own selfishness? Were you able to embrace your findings as growth opportunities? What might be going on under the surface that makes it difficult for the ego to let go? What does your ego feel it will lose in doing so?

- What is an area of your life in which you have a hard time surrendering to or even trusting in the Lord? Why do you think you have difficulties in those particular areas of your life?

- Have you ever had an experience of death and rebirth in your spiritual life? If so, have you encountered any similar processes in nature?

- How did you find the effort of being patient and forgiving with others at times when they seemed to be acting from a place void of love?

- Do you have any further reflections concerning this chapter?

DAY 1: LET THERE BE LIGHT

A wind from God swept over the face of the waters.
Then God said, "Let there be light"; and there was light.
And God saw that the light was good.

(Genesis 1:2–4)

The second verse of Genesis continues by indicating that long
before we ever become aware of it, the Spirit of God has been
surrounding us and hovering over us. How could divine love be
anything but always present with us? God is always waiting for
the moment we are ready and able to see the first rays of spiritual light. This is the first step of our spiritual evolution.

> God's omnipotence, omniscience, and omnipresence . . .
> come from divine love and divine wisdom much the way
> the sun's power and presence everywhere on earth come
> from the sun's heat and light. (*True Christianity* §49)

During the birth of our first biological child, the nurses sent
me out of the labor room because the procedure had become
complicated. I was wracked with anxiety about the safety of
my wife and child, so I went to an adjacent room and prayed,
knowing that I'd find out he was finally born when I heard the

screams of his first breath. When the staff raced down the hall, calling to each other with urgency, I rushed back in to find out what was happening. I was shocked to hear that Evan had already been born. Shovha, my wife, was safe, and the nurses directed me to a tiny incubator against the far wall of the room. The vision of my son's rich, brown eyes, still bluish from birth, as we gazed at each other through the Plexiglass will be forever alive in my memory. The awe and wonder I felt in that moment was unlike any other, due not only to the extreme tension that led up to his birth but also to his silent gaze. Stuck for hours in the birth canal, Evan's lungs had collapsed. Though I know that newborn eyes are unable to see clearly, I still feel that there was some kind of connection. Indeed, throughout his nine months spent in the womb, I felt a spiritual communication with my son that I cannot write off as mere imagination.

As profound as the moment was for me, my experience must have been minor when compared to that of Shovha, but Evan's experience was surely the most profound—among other things, he was seeing light for the first time in his life. I believe that his inability to cry must have had an enormous effect on those first seven minutes of his life outside the womb. Unable to hear his own screams, he stared out at me with what seemed to be serene, observant wonder. Even if newborns cannot breathe during those first minutes, the umbilical cord provides enough oxygen to keep them safe, so my son would not have been feeling the terror of asphyxiation. Not only does the alarming sound of their own crying perhaps distract newborns from seeing the wonder of light, but it is typical for them to close their eyes while crying. Thus, Evan's experience of life after birth was possibly more oriented toward "the seeing of light" than are most newborns' experiences.

In keeping with the foundational premise of this book— that all things of the natural world are reflections of spiritual reality—we, too, must be born as to our spirits, and that moment of spiritual birth is what is described in Genesis 1:3 when God says, "Let there be light."

Of all the symbols used to represent spiritual experience, *light* holds perhaps the most obvious meaning: intellectual truth. As we have seen, the metaphors woven into our everyday speech reveal to us that we intuit much more about spiritual reality than we realize: "A *light bulb* turned on in my head"; "I saw *the light*"; "It was an *enlightening* talk"; and "She *shed light* onto the situation." Buddha was *enlightened,* and Jesus said, "I am the light of the world" (John 8:12).

This light that is spoken of in various religious and spiritual traditions is the light of the spirit. It is the light that dispels the spiritual darkness into which we are born. This light, therefore, is in some sense the opposite of our prior state of darkness. It seems that spiritual truth very often in some way eludes normal logic. As already discussed, even though sense of self is the source of all evil, it is also the foundation upon which rests our spiritual life, our ability to give and receive love. And though part of spiritual awakening involves realizing that the self is an illusion, the way by which God evolves us includes what seems to be effort on our part from our sense of self—so much so that from within our subjective experience, there is no way around working hard to improve ourselves. According to Swedenborg:

> If we believed the way things really are, that everything good comes from the Lord and everything evil from hell, then we would not take credit for the good within us or blame for the evil. (*Heaven and Hell* §302)

> Since anything we do freely seems to be our own because it comes from our love (acting from our love is acting freely . . .), it follows that union with the Lord makes us feel that we have freedom and therefore identity; and the closer our union with the Lord, the greater our freedom and our identity. (*Divine Providence* §43)

Many of Jesus's words defy our logical expectations: in order not to be judged, we must not judge others; the last will be first, and the first will be last; having faith means working and serving. Similarly, when we are spiritually blind, we think we see; and when it dawns on us that we are spiritually blind, we are in fact seeing the light. Light is spiritual awareness and, in this case, the first dawn of spiritual awakening. It is a moment no less precious than the birth of a child, for that is truly what seeing the light is on a spiritual level.

Genesis 1 is not the only description of Creation found in the Bible:

> In the beginning was the Word, and the Word was with God, and the Word was God. He was in the beginning with God. All things came into being through him, and without him not one thing came into being. What has come into being in him was life, and the life was the light of all people. The light shines in the darkness, and the darkness did not overcome it. (John 1:1–5)

I find it interesting that both stories speak immediately about light in relation to creation. This story in John reveals that spiritual light is life—God's life—which is divine love. Thus, spiritual light is the first aspect of God that we are able to experience.

The first rays of light, however, don't always feel like love. Coming to understand our personal darkness is a painful process. We may suddenly have an insight into how much we take our spouse for granted, how judgmental and unforgiving we've been with our children, or how convicted by conscience we've been about illicit financial gain. Anytime we gain such insight into our own selfishness, a little bit of light enters into the darkness of our delusion.

When I was about eleven or twelve years old, I sang with the Philadelphia Boys Choir. I remember listening to a good friend from the choir talk about how much he hated his older brother who constantly bullied him. In that moment, I recognized how I, too, was often judgmental and harsh toward my younger brother and suddenly saw a void in my life where love should have been. The light shined in. For the first time, I genuinely *saw* and came to terms with the darkness that had been there all along. The light led to steady improvement in how I treated my brother. My parents had many times scolded me for being unkind to him, but I hadn't been ready to listen, let alone change. I didn't really see myself as having a problem—and that was the problem. Only in hearing the pain and hatred associated with a relationship that was not unlike my own did I become receptive of the light that God wished to shine into my life.

Based both on experiences of my own and those of others, it would seem that different elements of our character evolve at different times and at different rates. For example, while I had begun the process of improving as a brother, there were still plenty of other character defects about which I lacked the light of understanding until later. And I will always still need light. Surely, though, there is something special about our first exposure to spiritual light, because it induces a fundamental change in our lives that can't be undone: for the first time in our life, we realize that our own point of view is limited and that there is something higher than a life lived for the sake of selfhood. All subsequent insights into our many forms of selfishness are simply continuations of this first realization—that there are ugly elements of our character and they need to be dealt with.

Some people have enlightening experiences at the worst moments in their lives, such as, for example, when they hit the "rock bottom" of an addiction. Self-denial is a common element of addiction and is a good illustration of the darkness we all start in—denying the truth about ourselves is to live in darkness. But when we are no longer able to sustain the delusion that we have things in control—perhaps, for example, when the use of drugs or alcohol devastates our body or destroys our relationships with family and friends—the light begins to shine in. A harrowing experience with illness or a close encounter with death can also wake us up to leading a new life. Though these are dramatic examples of light shining into the darkness, moments of illumination often occur in more subtle ways. We may realize over a cup of coffee that our reasons for serving the church or helping out at a soup kitchen are motivated more by a desire to feel good about ourselves and look good in front of others than they are by a genuine interest in helping. Or we may watch a sunrise and realize that we have not been doing our part to help protect the environment. Such small moments of light are all around us.

One of Stephen W. Hawking's most celebrated theories is that black holes cannot sustain themselves; eventually, light is revealed and they in turn evaporate. I like to think of our emergence from spiritual darkness as paralleling this scientific theory. Selfish pursuits are, for multiple reasons, unsatisfying in the long run. The underlying reason, though, is that the pleasures of power, fame, wealth, and sensuality fade with time; they are inherently ephemeral. This being the case, our appetite for such pleasures ever increases and becomes insatiable. Because our sense of self is of the material body, which is bound in space and time, our pursuit of self-based delights and so-called "happiness" is also bound by these restrictions. This means that there will always be tension between our selfish desires and the obstacles presented by space and time to fulfilling them. Social expectations, for example, bar us from indulging in our self-based wishes. Lack of money also prevents us from a good number of earthly pursuits. More fundamentally, our desire for contentment is at heart a spiritual concern, and spiritual concerns cannot be satisfied with physical matter. Being creatures of space and time, the "happiness" of a selfish life doesn't seem sustainable to me; just as the black holes in outer space emit light and eventually collapse, the void that is our spiritual darkness is shone upon by the light of God and eventually the darkness is dispelled.

While some of the moments of light in my own life have been of a more intellectual nature, they nonetheless did away with some corner of the darkness and consequently made things change for the better. In my sophomore year at Grinnell College, I intentionally became an agnostic. If God were real, I decided, one should be able to search and find proof of his existence. So from a neutral position, I engaged in an all-out pursuit of proof. If I could not find proof of God, I thought, I will not believe in him. I did away with the faith I had built up that was based on the ideas of other people so that my mind, as far as is possible, could be without intellectual or emotional bias regarding spiritual matters.

At the time, I could not see the emotional roots beneath the intellectual doubt, but I now see the connection between my doubt and a state of void in my life. I saw so much chaos, trauma, and agony in the world that I was unable to trust life and therefore could not trust God. How could I trust, let alone love, God if he created this reality of suffering? Life seemed meaningless, at best, and quite possibly cruel. The teaching of an afterlife offered no comfort, as the hope of heaven was tainted by the idea that anyone might spend eternity in hell; besides, where was the proof for either? I wondered if love was actually a protective human delusion that coated over the terror of life's utter meaninglessness. This lack of trust in love was the void.

The resolution of this existential crisis came from a startling experience I had months later. As my search for intellectual proof of God became an obsession, I was eventually no longer controlling the search; the thoughts took over and spun through my mind day and night. By the time I went home for

Christmas break during that second year at Grinnell, I had been suffering tremendous mental tension. At home, I lay exhausted on the couch in the family room of my parents' house. After several minutes, I stood up from the couch, walked across the room, became dizzy, and then passed out behind the television in the corner. When I awoke on the couch, I was disoriented for several minutes. *How did I get back on the couch?* I looked around for somebody who might have carried me back, but nobody was around. Slowly it dawned on me that my collapse had been an extremely life-like waking dream.

I don't know what happened, but after this experience, my mind was still. The obsession to find proof of God was gone. It was as if that part of my mind collapsed and died behind the television. My doubt in God also died with that dream. According to Google Dictionary, a television is "a system for transmitting visual images." I cannot deny that a vision was transmitted to me through this dream—that my doubt in God could not be satisfied by the intellect. For months, I reached out to touch God, and though I found many reasonable arguments for his existence, I never did find that proof for which I searched. In finding nothing, I actually came to believe. I did not, however, arrive at this belief through any decision on my part; it just happened.

I see now that if God could be captured within the intellect and fully understood, he would be reduced to something akin to a "grand equation"—something mechanical. The intellect would have a vantage point higher than that of God and therefore one that stands above and beyond the Infinite. God would then not be God, as, by definition, he must transcend the boundaries created by intellectual proof. Had I succeeded at finding such intellectual proof, I would probably now be an atheist. I feel connected to Thomas, who refused to believe without tangible proof that Jesus had risen. Later, Jesus appeared and encouraged Thomas to touch the holes where the nails and spear had pierced him; in other words, Thomas was invited not to touch Jesus but to touch the space where Jesus was not. It was after this that Thomas exclaimed, "My Lord and my God!" (John 20:28) Like Thomas, I doubted God and demanded tangible proof. I reached out and felt empty space. And like Thomas, that experience led me to a powerful experience of God.

Suspension of preconceived notions was a kind of formlessness; disbelief in love was a void of sorts; and because of these things, it was a dark time in my life. This experience suggests that the dawning of light can occur on an intellectual level, dispelling darkness from our vision of reality, or on a volitional level, shining light onto manifestations of our selfishness and beginning the process of dispelling them.

Fundamentally, **Day 1** is about God's love shining into our lives to awaken us to some area of darkness that resides there. It is about insight. The first and most fundamental shining of light occurs when we realize that an egocentric life focused on self and in service of self is no life at all. It brings us neither joy nor peace and therefore prevents us from having good relationships with others. When immersed in self, we spend most of the time focused on the future; as a result, we feel dissatisfied, distracted, and frustrated with life. According to Swedenborg:

> [People in a state of innocence] have no anxiety about the future, but refer to anxiety about the future as "care for the morrow," which they say is pain at losing or not getting things that are not needed for their life's useful activities. (*Heaven and Hell* §278:2)

Even when we get what we want, the pleasure soon fades and we want more or something better. Ego-based living just doesn't work. When the light of this fact shines in, we begin to consider a different approach to living. The light has begun to penetrate the delusion, and the whole foundation of our mind begins to change. The evolution process has begun.

The Value of Contrast

And God separated the light from the darkness. God called
the light Day, and the darkness he called Night. And there was
evening and there was morning, the first day.

(Genesis 1:4–5)

One of the most wonderful results that comes from this new
light shining in our lives is that the darker aspects of our being begin to bless us rather than do us harm. No longer is the
darkness an all-enveloping void leaving our existence without
horizon. In relation to light, darkness functions as a catalyst
for progress. Just as the literal day and night mark the forward
motion of time, the alternating spiritual states of light and dark
are needed for the evolution of our spirit. So after we have experienced the blessing of light, our mind returns to the darkness of selfishness; but now the darkness, too, works as a blessing. We come to realize that there is something better than our
ordinary state of delusion. The darkness puts the light in stark
relief and in turn leaves us desiring that light and inspiring us
to search it out. The black-and-white Chinese symbol of the
yin and yang, which represents how opposites complement
each other, depicts this relationship. The cycle that produces
our forward spiritual motion is now in place.

The contrast that comes from our continual return to states
of darkness also works to soften up the ego by humbling us
before the mercy of God. If we were not to repeatedly de-
scend and were left in a permanent state of light, we'd end
up more self-centered than we were before. Our sense of self
would come to believe, "Aha, this is who I am! I'm really good!"
But the goodness that comes with the dawning of the light
has nothing to do with the self. The alternating states of dark
and light, night and day, help us to stay humble. Humility is
the foundation of spiritual progress, because only when we are
humble are we receptive of God.

Just as our alternating states of darkness and light humble us before the true source of our goodness, they also prevent our transformation from being too abrupt. Imagine if you woke up one day and found yourself instantaneously changed from selfish to completely unselfish. Such a sudden change would offer no sense of continuity from your prior state of darkness to your present state of light. You might begin to wonder who you really are. Life would probably begin feeling fake. Even worse, we might feel manipulated—so drastically altered and not of our own choosing that we might begin to blame God. Perhaps we would even resent God, deciding that the light of unselfishness is not worth the price of losing our selfhood completely. A loving God would never wish to rip away our sense of selfhood for the sake of a so-called perfect human being. And so the states of darkness must remain. Our spiritual evolution must occur gradually, organically.

On occasion, we do have powerful, life-altering spiritual experiences. After going through such an experience, such as near-death, we can enter into a depression. Friends of mine have had this experience, I have had it, and I've read authors who relate this experience. I believe this depression has to do with the sense of selfhood having difficulty in integrating the experience and in understanding its new role.

This process of going back and forth between states of darkness and light also increases our capacity to empathize with others. Having experienced both states, we are less likely to judge someone who is struggling with hostility, greed, lust, or arrogance; instead, we remember, "We're all human beings, and I've certainly been there myself." In demonstrating empathy and tolerance, we become more likely to forgive, to love, and to be of use in others' journeys.

When all is said and done, our continual return to states of selfishness is an inevitable part of being human. While a sense of selfhood will always entail some level of selfishness, which is a limitation to our ability to love, we must have that sense of selfhood in order to participate at all in the giving and receiving of love. The earth is able to support life because the momentum driving it away from the sun is constantly and perfectly balanced against the sun's gravity pulling it in. Similarly, our sense of self pushes us away from God, while God's infinite love is always pulling us in to create the exact balance needed for our spiritual evolution to occur.

> If the spiritual world's sun did not seem to be as far from angels as the physical world's sun is from us, the whole angelic heaven, the hell underneath it, and our globe of lands and seas below them could not be under the Lord's watchful guidance, omnipresence, omniscience, omnipotence, and providence. In the same way, if our world's sun were not at the distance from the earth where we see it to be, it could not be present and effective with its warmth and light in all our lands, so it could not provide its subsidiary resources to the spiritual world's sun. (*Divine Love and Wisdom* §106)

Our existence here on earth is messy—with its natural disasters, diseases, and decay—and it is also marked with the results arising from our selfishness, such as hatred, poverty, and war; but for the sake of life, this toll is acceptable.

It may seem strange that evening is mentioned before morning in both this verse from Genesis 1 and those that follow, but according to Hebrew tradition, which is based on the Creation story, the day begins at sundown. And from a spiritual perspective, it makes complete sense to mention evening first, as progress is characterized by our moving from darker to lighter states and from colder to warmer states. This is just another example of how the nature of our spiritual development is a reflection of the Word.

Witnessing the Light

One of the many privileges of working as a psychotherapist is that I am given the opportunity to witness light dawn into troubled lives. (Throughout this book, all descriptions of my practice as a psychotherapist—from the names of clients to the details of their cases—have been changed.) A woman by the name of Rita, for example, came to my office convinced that she would soon be dying of cancer after having a scare with what turned out to be a benign cyst. She had developed a delusional conviction that she either had or would come to have cancer; and as a result, her mind was gripped with obsessional thoughts about contracting this disease. Rita was so riddled with fear that she found it difficult to work. She compulsively searched websites for information about cancer and constantly checked her body for signs of its presence. She met with doctors repeatedly, and despite being told that nothing was wrong, she couldn't escape her obsession. Rita doubted the proficiency of her doctors and so sought out others. She worried so much about her health that she lost sleep, began having panic attacks, and developed hypochondriasis (hypochondria). Her obsession was eroding every aspect of her life, including her social life. It got to the point that she couldn't even answer the phone.

Rita was wholly convinced that her fears were well-founded and that she did *in fact* have cancer. Here we see the double delusion discussed in **Day 0** (pp. 26–27, above)—her primary delusion that she was sick was compounded by the delusion that her doctors were wrong and that she was right. According to Rita, it was just a matter of time before the disease manifested with discernible symptoms. Slowly, we reviewed the facts—the expert opinions, the different test results, and the fact that her behavior was perfectly consistent with hypochondriasis. Initially, regardless of the evidence in support of the fact that her problem was psychological and not medical, Rita remained convinced that her anxiety was justified. It seemed that the more I pushed, the less willing she was to consider the possibility.

As this cognitive approach that I was taking with Rita was not producing results, I decided to switch to person-centered therapy—an approach that was developed by Carl Rogers. By a process of trial and error, I came to realize the appropriateness of particular therapeutic approaches in relation to **Days 1, 2,** and **3** (the days of our spiritual evolution in which we are operating from under the delusion of selfhood). In this case, employing the cognitive approach was a bit premature, as it is more representative of **Day 2.** Person-centered therapy, on the other hand, relates quite clearly to **Day 1,** the stage of Creation in which "a wind from God [sweeps] over the face of the waters."

The focus of person-centered therapy is to create a completely safe environment for the client. With undivided attention and the entirety of his or her being, the therapist empathizes with the client and shows "unconditional positive regard" (i.e., love, described in a way that scientific journals could accept). The therapist works to create a tremendous amount of trust and safety through which light is able to dawn into the mind of the client and dispel forms of darkness that are harming his or her life. It is hard to see our own flaws, as doing so makes us feel weak, vulnerable, embarrassed, and just bad. This is why safety and emotional warmth are primary to a successful psychoeducational environment. I very much like Rogers's person-centered therapy; it is a true pleasure to attempt to create a safe and loving space in my office that allows healing light to dawn.

Person-Centered Therapy

Developed in the 1950s, elements of person-centered therapy have found their way into all forms of psychological therapy. In counseling, rapport is paramount. In fact, empirical evidence has shown that good rapport correlates with good outcome and bad rapport correlates with bad outcome, regardless of the approach. Person-centered therapy is all about rapport. Rogers was a master of rapport. One could even argue that his form of therapy is one and the same thing as developing great rapport.

Rogers believed that all people have a natural drive for self-realization, to evolve psychologically and become as healthy and productive as possible. He further believed that societal shortcomings often stifle this self-actualizing force, leading to psychological dysfunction. To avoid hampering the client's own self-actualizing potential in any way, Rogers never analyzed, prescribed, advised, instructed, or even answered questions! Somewhere inside, the client knows how to understand and solve his or her own problems. Rogers focused all of his attention onto the client, and he described this as entering some other kind of consciousness, somewhat like a trance. He listened and echoed back in his own words what the client was expressing, sometimes tying things together but always attempting to enter deeply into the mental reality of the client. Rogers cared less about the words themselves and more about the emotions behind the words. If the therapist could create safe enough emotional and social environments, he thought, the client would solve his or her own problems and heal by means of the self-actualizing drive. I like to think of the therapist in Rogers's person-centered therapeutic relationship as *sweeping,* or hovering, with love *over the face of the waters* that are the client's state, waiting for the client's self-actualizing potential to gain insight—to see the light—and resolve his or her problems.

Using person-centered therapy, it was not long before Rita was able to admit that *maybe* her problem was psychological in nature; and over time, she increasingly came to believe this to be the case until she finally understood that she was suffering from hypochondriasis. Here we see an instance of the first dawning of light, one in which Rita gained insight into the darkness of her former state. **Day 1** is about light penetrating the darkness that is our delusion of selfhood, a delusion that is characterized by an over-concern with self-preservation and an inability to trust anyone other than oneself. This is something we all have in common. The facts are plain: we do not always know what is best for us, least of all when our judgment is clouded by emotion.

For Rita, these characteristics were demonstrated by her fear of dying from cancer and by the fact that she placed her faith in her own ideas alone and was unable to accept expert opinions based on extensive testing. Rita was learning an important spiritual lesson: that *her* thoughts and feelings weren't always correct. In refusing to believe the insistent thoughts she was having about cancer, Rita was learning to focus less on herself, thereby both alleviating her hypochondriasis and helping her make steps toward greater humility. Hypochondriasis was destroying her life, making her miserable and unable to function. Love is life, so non-love is non-life. Because God is the source of all love and love is the source of all healing, that which gives life and facilitates long-term functioning and peace must be of God and so is spiritual to some degree.

Rita had a traumatic childhood, and a common reaction to trauma is an unconscious decision to protect one's self. A child can become hypervigilant about his or her safety to such a degree that the mind focuses constantly on the self and builds up a wall to block out anything that might compromise the child's safety—even expert medical opinions, which might induce the child to take a lax stance on his or her own safety and in turn allow danger to penetrate. My suggestions to Rita that maybe she didn't have cancer worked in just this way. She felt threatened by my opinions and as a result became more resistant. It was by simply allowing myself to do nothing but shine unconditional positive regard onto her that she felt safe enough to penetrate the walls built up by her trauma. It seems that forms of self-focus and self-obsession are simply responses to external factors—from trauma to everyday experiences to socialization to genetics to even the fact that we are born into space and time. Though we don't choose to be self-obsessed, it is our responsibility and salvation to work on liberating ourselves from such a state.

Another client, Celeste, had been physically abused at a very young age by her father. As a result, she learned to distrust people, especially those closest to her. Celeste loathed feeling powerless and vulnerable, so she wanted to push everyone away. Yet, at the same time, she was extremely needy for love— to know there was someone in her life whom she could trust. Need for love made her feel all the more vulnerable and weak. To overcome this feeling, she sought power in the way that she had first experienced it—by means of cruelty. She was trapped in a cycle.

With Celeste, we see something that I've become convinced is true of all disorders: a disorder, like a virus, takes possession of us and then self-perpetuates in a mechanical way; it hijacks us. Drug use is an excellent example. Having worked with many heroin addicts, I have witnessed how the drug hijacks the user's will until it is as if the drug is taking the drug. In a similar, intergenerational way, mental and physical abuses hijack us and self-perpetuate in a mechanical way to the next generation. A vicious downward cycle is set in place, and only with effort and awareness can we stop that cycle.

Celeste defended her broken heart and spirit by aiming her hostility at others. Doing so succeeded in giving her a new sense of strength and in making her feel protected, but it also pushed people away as she sank into even deeper loneliness. In order to protect the remnants of her self-esteem, she could *choose* to push people away rather than believe that they rejected her because of who she was. Ironically, in choosing to push people away, she was actually cementing that as part of who she was. Here, again, we see the mechanical hijacking of her true humanity.

When I first met Celeste, she would spend entire sessions swearing, shouting curses at life, and ranting about how she hated everything and everyone. She never considered that there might be something going on inside that made her life so unhappy. For a long time, I suggested to her that the problems she was experiencing weren't entirely on the outside and that her life would be better if she made a few changes, such as forgiving people and refraining from acts of hostility. I didn't get very far with her. For a person affected by trauma in the way Celeste was, advice and instructions are interpreted as criticism and rejection. This makes it difficult for them to learn or grow.

Celeste had a classic example of what is officially labeled as "borderline personality disorder," a term I strongly dislike because it seems condemning of a person's very identity. It leaves a person feeling not like they *have* a problem but like they *are* a problem. I would love to see this disorder renamed "chronic childhood trauma reactivity disorder," for example. This lays the blame where it belongs—on trauma. I've not met someone with this syndrome who was not traumatized as a child.

Cognitive behavioral therapy (CBT) is the favored approach today. It has been proven effective and is relatively quick, which insurance companies demand. In addition to Celeste, I have had a number of cases, though, in which after it became clear that CBT was going nowhere, I fell back on person-centered therapy with amazing results. Just as I did with Rita, I eventually switched tactics and just listened to Celeste's hostility. If and when there was a pause, I'd echo back the emotions that I heard, empathizing with the pain and anger she expressed. It didn't take long for this "sweeping" tolerance and unconditional positive regard to have an effect. She began to recognize her own mistakes and unhelpful attitudes. It was almost miraculous. Celeste's wounds are deep, and she still has a long way to go, but she made wonderful progress.

It took a considerable amount of time for the young Celeste to understand (or at least admit to herself) that some of the problems she was experiencing were arising from within her and that her appraisal of everyone and everything as being horrible may not have been entirely accurate. This understanding was able to occur only in the safe social environment of unconditional love, one without the presence of active suggestions, instructions, or advice. It was the first ray of light needed to begin the long process of redefining herself and her life.

I like to think of the unconditional positive regard, unfiltered empathy, and undivided attention espoused by Rogers as our attempt to embody or even channel the same kind of love that God constantly pours out into us. That we are given to do this by virtue of God's love in a way that feels as if we ourselves are doing the loving is the crowning gift among all graces. In a book I read a long time ago (I can't recall the title or author), the author describes his belief that God, as pure love, constantly pours himself out into creation so completely that he is one with creation and without a selfhood other than this love that is intrinsically united with that which is loved. This is a perfect kind of empathy, one I see in Jesus's words that what we do to others, we do to him (Matthew 25:40). God is always sweeping over us with his pure love, waiting for that moment when we are ready for the light of understanding to dawn in our hearts and minds with profound effects.

SUGGESTED PRACTICES

The chief message of this chapter is that the first dawn of spiritual light into our lives includes a heartfelt perception of the darkness within and the need for God's loving mercy and grace. Seeing our own darkness allows us to desire, seek after, and strive for more light and a purpose higher than the self. This chapter is also about the fact that in giving unconditional love, we may help others in this first step of spiritual evolution.

Cultivating Awareness in Daily Activities

1

During the **Day 1** period, notice the delicate, gentle beauty of light. Spend time just sitting and absorbing the wondrous radiance that is the light of the sun. Consider its significance as a symbol in our spiritual lives.

The Lord sheds light into our lives every day. It may seem like a relatively small thing. For example, we may have the urge to criticize someone, but the voice of conscience stops us; or it may be that we are tempted to eat something unhealthy but refrain from doing so in an effort to love and respect our body. Try noticing a moment of light as you go about your day. Note that it does not need to be in relation to a behavior or a thought. Instead, you might gain a new insight about the Lord, the Word, or some other spiritual matter.

2

Throughout the next few days, consider whether there are any current states of darkness in your life. Observe what possible factors—perhaps social forces, unhealthy views or beliefs, family patterns, lack of faith, etc.—work to sustain these states of darkness. By examining these states, we begin to let God's light shine upon the darkness. Notice how these dark states negatively impact our life—our social relationships, our mood, our outlook. We are seeing these states of darkness for what they are and so are getting closer to moving beyond the lies that sustain them.

Meditative Practice

This meditation is designed to serve as a window through which God's light might shine into your mind. Darkness and light are intimately and inevitably bound to one another. That they have any meaning at all demands this relationship; without both, neither has meaning. In the **Day 0** meditation, we observed thoughts and considered to what extent those thoughts arose from the illusion of self. Simply noticing thoughts in this way helps usher light into our minds—to notice darkness is to gain light. The purpose of *this* chapter's meditation is not just to identify darkness but also to actively invite the living spiritual light of God into our lives. I have found that entering the roles of characters in the Bible has proven a very effective way of encountering the Lord, so we will use a story from the Bible as part of our meditation.

Just like the induction for the first two chapters, the following induction serves to gather attention inward, to relax both mind and body, to bring about a sense of oneness, and to prepare one for meditation. However, this induction serves the further purpose of drawing awareness to God and inviting the mind to sense oneness with God's loving presence. It does this by using the image of warm, fluid, healing light entering the body. Since the dawning of light is the beginning of our spiritual evolution, it would seem appropriate to use the second induction to introduce the meditations for **Days 1** through **7** (pp. 63, 88, 112, 135, 152, 175, and 187, below).

Meditation Induction 2

After getting into your meditation position, make any necessary adjustments to become comfortable and relaxed.

[Pause for a moment]

Begin by focusing on the sensation of the breath moving in and out through your nose ... in and out ... in and out ... in and out.

[Pause for 15 seconds]

Now, visualize a golden, fluid light that flows in and out with each breath. Let this light be the presence of the Divine.

[Pause for 5 seconds]

Breathe the light slowly and deeply in, and then imagine a small glowing sphere forming in the center of your chest. Now, slowly breathe out.

[Pause for 5 seconds]

Slowly breathe in the warm, living light, noticing as the sphere grows larger. Now, hold the breath ... and breathe out.

[Pause for 5 seconds]

Again, slowly and deeply breathe in the living, peace-giving light, letting the sphere fill the entire area of your chest. Now, hold the breath ... and slowly let it go.

[Pause for 5 seconds]

Breathing normally, sense the light flow in with each inhalation. See the sphere of light as it continues to fill your chest and then begins to glow outward into the space around your chest.

[Pause for 10 to 15 seconds]

Now, deeply inhale this living, golden light and hold it. Feel its warmth create peace in your chest. Now, gently breathing out, feel the light moving down through your

*abdomen, through your legs, and into your feet, filling your
feet with warm peace.*

[Slight pause]

Breathe in the light deeply.

[Slight pause]

*Breathing out, feel the light flow down and fill your
lower legs with peace and warmth.*

[Pause for 5 seconds]

Breathe in deeply and hold it.

[Pause briefly again]

*Breathing out slowly, sense the light flowing down to fill
your upper legs so that your entire legs are now filled with
the living light of God's love.*

[Slight pause]

Breathe in the light.

[Pause again]

*Breathing out, sense the light as it flows into your pelvic
region, filling it with warmth and utter peace.*

[Pause for several seconds]

Breathing in, the light rejoins the sphere in your chest.

[Slight pause]

*Breathing out, the light flows down to fill your belly so
that your body from your chest to your feet is now full of living, healing, peace-giving light. Stay with this feeling.*

[Pause for several seconds]

Breathing in, the light rejoins the sphere.

[Pause]

Breathing out, the light flows through your shoulders and then down through your arms, filling your fingers and palms.

[Pause for several seconds]

Breathing in, the light rejoins the sphere.

[Momentary pause]

Breathing out, the light flows into your wrists, forearms, elbows, and upper arms.

[Pause for several seconds]

Breathe in deeply and slowly.

[Momentary pause]

Breathing out, the light flows up along your spine, through the back of your neck, and up over the back of your head; it then spills over your forehead and face, filling everything from your neck up.

[Slight pause]

Breathe in and hold it.

[Pause for a few seconds]

Breathing out, the light from the sphere radiates throughout your whole body, bringing living peace and calm to your entire being.

[Pause for a few seconds]

In the quiet that follows, breathe normally, entering further into this sensation of peace and calm.

[Pause for 2 minutes; then begin the appropriate chapter's meditation]

Meditation—**Day 1:** Let There Be Light

In a contemplative way, we will now read from John 9, paying particular attention to the significance of the blind man and noticing the parallels between this chapter of the Bible and the very beginning of Genesis. During the reading, gently enter into the life of the blind man as deeply as possible. Putting yourself in his place, patiently and deliberately move through the story as best you can, seeing what he sees, hearing what he hears, and feeling what he feels. As the words are spoken, consider each character of the story to be an element of your own mind. Each of us has a variety of inner dispositions—some parts of our mind believe, while others doubt; some yearn to see, while some are too blind to even yearn—but amidst all of these differences, God is somehow always present, gently entering into our life.

[Pause for 15 seconds]

Before we begin, from within this meditative state, let us pray for a few moments that God's spiritual light will illumine his Word.

[Pause for 1 minute; then read the following]

From John 9:
As he walked along, he saw a man blind from birth. His disciples asked him, "Rabbi, who sinned, this man or his parents, that he was born blind?" Jesus answered, "Neither this man nor his parents sinned; he was born blind so that God's works might be revealed in him. We must work the works of him who sent me while it is day; night is coming when no one can work. As long as I am in the world, I am the light of the world." When he had said this, he spat on the ground and made mud with the saliva and spread the mud on the man's eyes, saying to him, "Go, wash in the pool of Siloam" . . . Then he went and washed and came back able to see.

[Pause for 15 seconds]

The neighbors and those who had seen him before as a beggar began to ask, "Is this not the man who used to sit and beg?" Some were saying, "It is he." Others were saying, "No, but it is someone like him." He kept saying, "I am the man." But they kept asking him, "Then how were your eyes opened?" He answered, "The man called Jesus made mud, spread it on my eyes, and said to me, 'Go to Siloam and wash.' Then I went and washed and received my sight." They said to him, "Where is he?" He said, "I do not know."

They brought to the Pharisees the man who had formerly been blind. Now it was a sabbath day when Jesus made the mud and opened his eyes. Then the Pharisees also began to ask him how he had received his sight. He said to them, "He put mud on my eyes. Then I washed, and now I see." Some of the Pharisees said, "This man is not from God, for he does not observe the sabbath." But others said, "How can a man who is a sinner perform such signs?" And they were divided.

[Pause for 15 seconds]

So they said again to the blind man, "What do you say about him? It was your eyes he opened." He said, "He is a prophet." . . .

For the second time they called the man who had been blind, and they said to him, "Give glory to God! We know that this man is a sinner." He answered, "I do not know whether he is a sinner. One thing I do know, that though I was blind, now I see." They said to him, "What did he do to you? How did he open your eyes?" He answered them, "I have told you already, and you would not listen. Why do you want to hear it again? Do you also want to become his disciples?" Then they reviled him, saying, "You are his disciple, but we are disciples of Moses. We know that God has spoken to Moses, but as for this man, we do not know where he comes from." The man answered, "Here is an astonishing thing! You do not know where he comes from, and yet he opened my eyes. We know that God does not listen to sinners, but he does listen to one who worships him and obeys his will. Never since the world began has it been heard that anyone opened the eyes of a person born blind. If this man were not from God, he could do nothing."

[Pause for 15 seconds]

They answered him, "You were born entirely in sins, and are you trying to teach us?" And they drove him out.

Jesus heard that they had driven him out, and when he found him, he said, "Do you believe in the Son of Man?" He answered, "And who is he, sir? Tell me, so that I may believe in him." Jesus said to him, "You have seen him, and the one speaking with you is he." He said, "Lord, I believe." And he worshiped him.

[Pause for 15 seconds]

ooooo

Now that you have had a chance to walk in the blind man's shoes, repeat the following mantra with each breath, entering the meaning of the words as fully and genuinely as you can: Breathing in, say to yourself, "Lord, please . . ." Breathing out, say, "Enlighten me . . ."

[Pause for 15 seconds]

In the quiet that follows, breathe in and out slowly and deeply.

Doing Practice

Try allowing yourself to facilitate the Lord's desire to shed light into the lives of others: listen to someone with your entire attention and with unconditional positive regard. You may also wish to share with someone your own experiences of spiritual light and the insights that you may have gained. You may wish to offer "sweeping" love by performing a selfless gesture for another.

Suggested Questions for Pondering and/or Discussion

- What was it like to spend time appreciating the light of the sun?

- Think about a moment of light that has occurred in your life or in the life of someone you know. What are some of the changes that have come about as a result of that moment of light? Have you had experiences similar to that moment of light? If so, what realizations did you have?

- What did you experience when reading and meditating on the Word? Did you gain any insights?

- Think about the states of darkness that you have experienced in your life. When did they begin? For how long did they last? What external factors or events in your life may have contributed to these states? What false thoughts may have sustained them? How do these states influence such things as your behavior, your relationships, your emotional state, and your self-esteem? What makes it difficult to let the light shine in?

- Since our continual returning to the darkness offers a contrast to our more desired states of light, the darkness actually inspires us to make efforts to move *toward* those states of light. The darkness also gives us perspective, both humbling us and making us more empathetic to the needs of others. Can you think of any times in your life when being in the darkness served you in such positive ways? What was it like trying to allow the Lord to shine his light through you for the sake of others?

- Do you have any further reflections concerning this chapter?

DAY 2: RISING ABOVE IT

And God said, "Let there be a dome in the midst of the waters, and let it separate the waters from the waters." So God made the dome and separated the waters that were under the dome from the waters that were above the dome. And it was so. God called the dome Sky. And there was evening and there was morning, the second day.

(Genesis 1:6–8)

Water is wondrous, beautiful, magical. Morning mist rises up to meet the sun and falls again to love the land and quench its thirst. It cleans away the dust from the leaves and grime from the cities. It is the rolling river, the throbbing sea, and the delicate crystalline snowflake that floats down to the ground. It is the sustainer of all life. The many manifestations and functions of water offer clues about its symbolic meaning. Water is often mentioned in the Bible, but unlike some other symbols, its meaning is explicitly given:

> For my thoughts are not your thoughts, nor are your ways my ways, says the Lord. For as the heavens are higher than the earth, so are my ways higher than your ways and my thoughts than your thoughts.

> For as the rain and the snow come down from heaven,
> and do not return there until they have watered the earth,
> making it bring forth and sprout, giving seed to the sower
> and bread to the eater, so shall my word be that goes out
> from my mouth; it shall not return to me empty, but it
> shall accomplish that which I purpose, and succeed in the
> thing for which I sent it. (Isaiah 55:8–11)

In the above passage, the Lord compares his Word to the rain that descends upon the earth and causes its fields to yield a rich harvest. Just as the words we use are expressions of our thoughts, the Word of God is the expression of his thoughts. So from the total context, we can sum up the message: while the Lord's thoughts are higher than our own, the Word of God as spiritual truth descends from heaven, providing spiritual nourishment and allowing us to live a productive life of love—just as rain descends from the sky and turns seeds into fruitful plants.

And here, the Lord compares his spirit to the life-giving water that feeds the land:

> For I will pour water on the thirsty land, and streams
> on the dry ground; I will pour my spirit upon your de-
> scendants, and my blessing on your offspring. They shall
> spring up like a green tamarisk, like willows by flowing
> streams. (Isaiah 44:3–4)

Jesus's words, too, indicate that water is a symbol of God's spirit or of the true vision of reality that enters us and inspires us with love to do good:

> Those who drink of the water that I will give them will
> never be thirsty. The water that I will give will become in
> them a spring of water gushing up to eternal life. (John
> 4:14)

Let anyone who is thirsty come to me, and let the one who believes in me drink. As the scripture has said, "Out of the believer's heart shall flow rivers of living water." (7:37–38)

When the Spirit of truth comes, he will guide you into all the truth; for he will not speak on his own, but will speak whatever he hears, and he will declare to you the things that are to come. (16:13)

And this helps us to understand the relationship between water and the Spirit of truth.

The Spirit of Truth

The Spirit of truth, or Word of God (Logos), can be a difficult concept to understand, but I interpret it to mean a spiritual perspective based on knowledge of God that transcends and liberates us from a merely natural perspective. From this perspective, selfless love is given priority over natural concerns, such as the acquisition of money or power. Seeing situations from a perspective of selfless love will cause us to bear spiritual fruit. Rather than getting angry when we are somehow insulted or treated poorly, we foster forgiveness. Rather than trying to exalt ourselves, we try to serve others. Rather than feeling the need to outdo others, we appreciate their successes. These are the fruit born of the Spirit of truth.

In Psalms, we read that if we meditate on God's law day and night, we will be like a tree planted by the rivers of water that thrives regardless of its circumstances:

Happy are those who do not follow the advice of the wicked, or take the path that sinners tread, or sit in the seat of scoffers; but their delight is in the law of the Lord, and on his law they meditate day and night. They are like trees planted by streams of water, which yield their fruit in its season, and their leaves do not wither. In all that they do, they prosper. (Psalm 1:1–3)

God's Word, which is to say God's thought, is like a river of water. If we meditate on God's truth, the Spirit of truth, it fills us with peace and fruitfulness that remains, regardless of our circumstances.

Living Water, or the Water of Life

The book of Revelation states that within the holy city of the new Jerusalem is "the river of the water of life, bright as crystal, flowing from the throne of God and of the Lamb" (Revelation 22:1). The river feeds the tree of life, allowing it to bear fruit all twelve months of the year. This clear water is flowing out from God; it is his Word, his truth, his thoughts made manifest to us. It is God's consciousness flowing into our own. Again, when our mind is able to absorb the Spirit of truth, we become enduringly fruitful. It is no coincidence that the next day of Creation (**Day 3**) entails the development of trees and other vegetation.

The water of life is the *living water* mentioned in John. This water represents the Spirit of truth, not the natural, clunky ideas about God that come about as a result of merely memorizing Bible verses. The water of life *is* the essence of truth, fluid and alive within us, guiding our thoughts, words, and actions. Just as does water in the natural world, the water of life is able to adapt to any given situation; it is a mutable form of consciousness that descends from the Divine and so approximates a true perspective on reality. As the quote from Psalms indicates and as has been supported by both my experience and the experiences of many others, meditation on the Word fills the mind with the living water of spiritual truth, which helps lift us up into a more spiritual, undisturbed state of mind. I do not mean to imply that meditation can instantly elevate a person permanently above selfishness and his or her natural perspective. Instead, meditation can raise a person above a lower baseline and, with time, slowly raise that baseline. In addition to single-minded, quiet focus on the written Word, we can also meditate on the spiritual truth that lies hidden within the natural universe—the evolving revelation of God's love that is present every step of the way.

The water of life is described as "bright as crystal," but not all waters are crystal-clear. Similarly, not all thoughts are based in truth. We have a wide variety of states of consciousness, just as water can appear in many different states. They can be icy, or void of the warmth of love. Sometimes they leap down from high mountains with the joy of the spirit; sometimes they stagnate in bogs of self-pity or murky pools of resentment; and sometimes they fill up with the tumultuous waves of upset. Our thoughts can rise up like mists of prayer and meditation, and they can rain down with higher truths that bring about fruitfulness in our lives. Both water and consciousness are fluid and mutable. Our colloquial language also reveals the intuitive relationship between water and consciousness. We use such terms as *stream of consciousness, brainstorming, foggy-mindedness,* and *a flood of thought* to describe our thinking; we refer to our inspiration as being *all dried up* and to our mood as *stormy.*

Just as our body thirsts for clean water to drink, our spirit thirsts for clarity of thoughts and feelings. A clear understanding about God and the things of the spirit also provides the tools we need to clean up our act. When we realize that God's love for us is so great that he is willing to suffer and die for our sake, we are inspired to love others. When we realize that loving others is incompatible with some selfish habit, we gain spiritual perspective and begin to alter our lifestyle. Like the waters of baptism, the truth of God's infinite love allows us to wash ourselves clean.

The Waters Under and Above the Dome

In the Bible, when we read about waters, we can understand them to represent forms of consciousness, good or bad depending on the context and qualities of the waters mentioned. This leads us to a better understanding of the meaning of Genesis 1:6–8, wherein God divides the waters above the dome from the waters below the dome. According to Swedenborg:

> The inner self is called the [*dome*], the knowledge in the inner self is called the [*waters that were above the dome*], and the facts belonging to the outer self are called the [*waters that were under the dome*].
>
> Before we are reborn, we do not know even that an inner being exists, let alone what it is, imagining there is no difference between the two selves. This is because we are absorbed by bodily and worldly interests and merge the concerns of the inner being with those interests. Out of distinct and separate planes we make one dim, confused whole. . . .
>
> We begin to notice while being reborn . . . that the inner self exists. We become aware that the attributes of the inner self are good feelings and true ideas, which are the Lord's alone. (*Secrets of Heaven* §24:1–2, 3)

This describes how the Word of God raises some of our thoughts up from the ego-immersed consciousness that makes up the waters below. We can understand this dome, or expansive space, that God creates between the waters above and the waters below as that place wherein we gain a little space from our own thinking. There, we have a new, higher perspective from which to observe the turbulent waters of our own lower, selfish forms of consciousness.

Before, we had no ability to rise up above our own thinking; our consciousness was fully immersed in all of the thoughts that entered our mind, being tossed about like an abandoned raft at sea. Now rather than being lost in a sea of emotions, desires, and consequent ego-based thoughts, we are one step removed. We still have negative thoughts, but we are no longer completely controlled by them. We still feel anxiety, resentment, pride, desire, and all of the other ego-based states of mind, but we are not inundated by them; they are not the *only* states of mind we have. This meta-consciousness allows us to discern the quality of the thoughts that flow through our mind. Now we are given to stop and think: "Is this thought true?" "Is this thought valuable?" "Are these thoughts coming from a higher perspective?" "Are these thoughts immersed in egoic concerns?"

So if the space between the waters represents detached observation of consciousness, the waters above represent new, higher, spirit-based thinking. When we were in the dark of the waters below, we viewed life in terms of what we can get out of it. Our ego-based sense of justice was "an eye for an eye." Our ego-based idea of love was "I'll love those who love me." Once we begin observing and evaluating our old ways of thinking, a new consciousness and conscience begins to take shape. For example, when once we may have held onto resentment or engaged in verbal combat, we might now be able to rise above those behaviors and in turn let them go. These higher ways of thinking do not naturally arise within us—from our sense of selfhood—but must come from the living waters above.

Jesus teaches that we should love our enemies; that we should lay down our lives for others; that we should give of our abundance to the needy; that we should forgive seventy times seven times; that we should take the lowly seat; that if we lust, we commit adultery; that we should refrain from worrying about what we will eat and wear. Teachings such as these enter our mind and open us to the waters above, to higher forms of consciousness than those we knew before. The waters above are raining down and nourishing our spirit: "The attributes of the inner self are good feelings and true ideas, which are the Lord's alone."

Because these teachings are completely contrary to what is typically our ego-based mindset, they are not yet central to our being. We start to see them, but they are still "up there." We begin to notice the differences between emotions resulting from ego-consciousness and those that come from God-consciousness. The former brings us fleeting pleasures and the excitement that comes with self-advancement in the material world, but ultimately ego-consciousness always sinks us back into churning waves of dissatisfaction. The latter, on the other hand, gives us a subtle, more enduring inner peace and calm—a respite from the insatiable slave-master, our ego.

When we understand the story of Creation as a parable relating to our spiritual evolution, the message of **Day 2** follows seamlessly from that of **Day 1**. In the first day, we see the light, recognizing that we have been living from and for the ego and that doing so is harmful to both ourselves and those around us. In seeing the light, we see that we have been in darkness. Just as light shows us how objects are situated around us in the physical world, insight into our darkness begins to show us how our mind is typically situated in a state of self-absorption. This new insight gives us pause, and we begin to reflect on our values, beliefs, and attitudes. We begin to notice our mind from within a new mental space. This space is the dome (also referred to as the firmament or the expanse) that God makes during the second day of Creation. And the waters coming from above make up the beginnings of our new spirit-based consciousness. Furthermore, just as the light of dawn draws up mist from the surface of a lake, our early spiritual insights begin to draw our thoughts upward from the surface of the waters below.

God called the dome Sky—or in other words, *heaven.* This elevated mental space that the dome provides truly is heaven, because it gives us separation and peace from our lower mind.

Again, we read that the evening and the morning make up the second day. Just as it did with the first day, this means that we are moving from a lower state, *evening*, up to a higher state, *morning*.

Cognitive Therapy

If Carl Rogers's person-centered therapy mirrors God's sweeping, or hovering, over us on the first day of Creation, then Aaron Beck's cognitive therapy reflects the essence of the second day of Creation, wherein God makes for us a mental space from which we gain perspective on our delusional states. The goal of cognitive therapy is to observe one's own thoughts, to notice those thoughts that hinder our well-being, and then to replace those harmful thoughts with more accurate and positive thoughts that can raise us up above our prior problematic states of mind. These negative thoughts are usually automatic and constantly flowing through the mind; without making a concerted effort, they go unnoticed. For example, automatic thoughts that typically accompany depression are: *I'm worthless. Nothing I do works out. Everyone hates me. I'll never get better. What's the point in trying?* The common thread found throughout these thoughts is that they make absolute negative pronouncements, using terms like *nothing, everyone,* and *never.* Such thoughts are untrue and unproductive, but they will reign strong if not consciously deposed. While these thoughts don't immediately seem to be born of selfishness, they are solidly egoic in that one's mood is based on evaluation of self and self-based evaluation of reality.

Cognitive therapy was first developed in relation to depression, and it has proven to be as effective as medication. Whether depressed or not, we all have egoic automatic thoughts. One of the most common and most unnoticed forms of automatic thinking is the ongoing inner dialogue of judgment. Unless we apply conscious effort to observe and separate from the lower mind, we likely spend much of our time on an imaginary throne of judgment. We see someone wearing three rings through their eyebrow and say to ourselves that they are foolish. We judge a stranger in a three-piece suit as being "part of the system." We judge liberals and conservatives; we judge other drivers; we judge the day as being good or bad based on the weather; we judge ourselves, our kids, our spouse, or all three for not living up to our expectations; we judge life for not being the way we want it to be; and we judge God for making life the way it is!

Judgment is a great way to destroy happiness. When I judge other drivers, I am sure to be angry and resentful, a feeling that will taint the rest of my day. On the other hand, when I make a concerted effort *not* to judge other drivers and use the rise of anger as a signal to pray for them, I feel peace. When I judge my spouse, I feel sullen and resentful; when I refuse to judge, I feel fine. When I judge life and God, I soon find myself in a dark pit. The only thing I should judge is judgment itself. I must choose to let God be the only judge.

Automatic thinking is not limited to our more obvious negative thoughts; it is associated with other things as well, such as dissatisfaction and unrealistic desires. *I need this promotion. I need that car. I need Mr. Right. I need that girl. I need to be perfect.* Hardly ever are such "needs" representative of true thinking, and they certainly aren't conducive to well-being. So rather than saying *I need to make my mark on the world*, we should perceive the truth and say instead, *I will do my best to bless this world. I need a piece of cake* becomes *The lower mind is craving cake, but taking care of my body is important, so I'll pass.* These types of thoughts can be difficult to counter, though, because the feeling of wanting something is a derivative of the desire that is central to who we are. As Swedenborg notes:

> There are many forms of love that have been given their
> own names because they are derivatives, such as desires,

cravings, appetites, and their gratifications and delights. (*Divine Love and Wisdom* §363)

But by rising up to that heavenly mental space and gaining some separation from the roaring waves of the lower mind, we can realize that these derivative feelings of need are not actually who we are. Instead, we are vessels created for genuine love: "Love is our life" (*Divine Love and Wisdom* §1).

Automatic thoughts loop through the mind over and over and we become convinced that they are true. Advertisers know that bombarding people with the same message will make them more susceptible to that message. With its relentless barrage of ego-oriented messages, our ego warps our sense of reality. When we have been judging others for a long time, we become entrenched in the idea that the judgment is justified. When thoughts constantly tell us we are worthless, we come to believe it. The same is true for thoughts that inflate our worth, that justify our mistakes, and that focus on feelings of need.

Self-glorification and self-justification are two other types of automatic thinking that arise from the lower mind. Self-glorification includes thoughts such as *I do so much for this community; I'm so good; I'm better than her; I'm a man, so I'm not going to do the housework; I'm so smart; I'm so beautiful;* and *I'm so accomplished.* With self-justification, a thief might say *I stole that Bible because God's Word should be available to all freely* (I was amazed to find out that the Bible was the most often stolen book!); an alcoholic might say *I deserve a little break from being sober, and I don't drink that much anyway;* and others of us might say things like *That's not my problem; someone else can deal with it.*

A cognitive therapist helps the client to identify automatic thoughts. Then, together, they analyze these thoughts to identify any elements that are simply untrue (e.g., that one is absolutely worthless). The client and therapist then create true and accurate thoughts to replace the old, unhelpful ones. I helped a client replace the thought *I'm a terrible mother* with *I did the best I could and provided a better childhood for my children than I received as a girl; My children's love for me shows that I did a good job;* and *Yes, I made some mistakes, but so do all people.* In progressively adopting these new narratives, that particular client's mood correspondingly improved.

I encourage clients to assume the best for their future, because optimism leads to happiness and productivity. I also encourage them to develop a faith or philosophy that inspires them with positive feelings, productive activities, and a sense of purpose. If an idea or attitude leads to productivity, happiness, and generosity, then that idea must be a true one, regardless of whether it is taken at face value to be preposterous.

The Christian belief that Jesus was born of a virgin, was the incarnation of God, and then died and rose again, for example, is a ludicrous proposition to the sense- and science-based mind. Yet belief in this vision of reality has been shown to increase well-being; it has certainly blessed *my* life beyond measure. Jesus also inspires us to turn away from our lower mind and to love one another. When I work with clients, I invite them to explore and redefine the meaning of truth, away from what is empirically proven in favor of what yields good fruit. It has been shown that people who have an active faith, for example, tend to be happier and even live longer. But while nearly all faith traditions involve ideas and beliefs that are logically absurd, I subscribe to the idea offered by Jesus: "The tree is known by its fruit" (Matthew 12:33).

Conversely, if a fact supposed to be truth diminishes our experience of life, then for me it is simply a fact and not a truth at all. For example, a study uncovered the fact that pessimists gauge measurements more accurately than do optimists. But if an optimist feels more satisfied with a half-full glass of water than a pessimist does with a half-empty glass, who's to say which measurement is the "true" measurement? The only thing this study reveals to me is that we should not let measuring devices dictate the parameters of reality! Improving subjective experience is more important to me than hard, cold measurement.

Seeing Our Automaticity

Danielle had a constant barrage of self-deprecating thoughts, many of which were more extreme than those of other depressed clients with whom I've worked. One of these thoughts was that she wasn't actually human. After we began investigating this thought, she stated that of course she knew she was human; but while immersed in the undifferentiated seas of depression, she *felt* inhuman. We developed a list of counter-thoughts, or positive replacement thoughts, one for each of her negative and untrue automatic thoughts. This work offered Danielle a chance to get her head above the waters below and look up toward the clouds of hope. She later reported, with good humor, that she was no longer struggling with feeling inhuman. Though primarily psychological, such healings also have a spiritual element. Knowing she was human improved her functionality and ability to interact positively with others, which is spiritual progress.

With all of the mental disorders I've encountered, there is always a level of self-absorption involved. This can actually be a blessing. All of us are born self-absorbed, but those suffering emotionally and mentally are presented with a uniquely overt opportunity to escape the delusions of self-absorption. The self-absorption of those who are suffering frequently manifests itself differently from that expressed by those without diagnosed psychological problems. In the case of depression, sufferers tend to focus on themselves—in particular, on their worthlessness—or make the fatalistic claim that life is bad. Such a claim reveals their belief that the self is able and entitled to make these wholesale judgments. Ironically, having such an ability and entitlement contradicts their supposed worthlessness; and this irreconcilability can shed some light on the fact that neither are they worthless nor is life bad.

I tell my clients that depression is a dictator with a powerful propaganda program. The overthrowing of that dictator is not a quick and easy process; but the first step is to start noticing the propaganda for what it is—lies—and then to reject it on that basis. One particular lie in this dictator's propaganda program is the idea of needing to be perfect. Again, though depression is an attack on one's sense of self-worth, it also involves a strange sense of self-inflation; in this case, the dictator entertains the possibility that the self could be perfect. A useful analogy here is that working on improving mental and behavioral habits is like weeding a garden. The goal isn't to prevent all weeds from sprouting ever again—they will always sprout up! The goal is to continually pull weeds, knowing that this effort will eventually reduce the total number of weeds at any given time, thereby increasing the health of the flowers of our life.

Another analogy I like to use is that our minds are like train stations and our thoughts are the trains. I like to joke that the depressed mind has a train called *I'm worthless and unlovable* that arrives every ten minutes, right on schedule, with a destination sign that reads "MISERY." This train always comes, but we can choose not to board it. By stepping back into the expansive dome, or sky, we can decide not to take that train of thought. From this new perspective, we are then able to request that the *I'm a valuable and lovable person* train with the "PEACE AND HAPPINESS" destination sign be sent to our train station. As the automatic thoughts of judgment and dissatisfaction are in great demand, they keep a tight schedule, so new trains don't realize that they are needed; we have to keep calling for these trains of counter-thought until it is assumed that they are in demand.

Driven by the Past

Cognitive therapy is useful for treating other psychological disorders as well. Another client of mine found it impossible to study. He had been an excellent student his entire life until he joined law school, where he found that he was unable to do anything but play video games, hang out with his friends, and spend time with his girlfriend. He repeatedly failed his tests and slipped several years behind his classmates. Finally, he decided to come for counseling. He must have "seen the light" that something was wrong—**Day 1** in his spiritual evolution on this particular matter.

This young man had been placed in a boarding school when he was in first grade. From ages six to eighteen, his every activity was dictated by outside forces. He had no choice in when he woke or when he slept, when he ate or what he ate, when he studied or when he played (and play time was sadly minimal). Little wonder that once on his own, his unconscious mind decided to catch up with his lost childhood, driving him to play when he should have been studying. Having had no executive power over his own life up to that point, he was ill-equipped to temper this strong drive to have fun. Before therapy, he did not have enough mental space to gain a third-person perspective on his mind. After our conversations together showed him how his past was driving his behavior, though, he gained the mental space he needed; the expansive dome was created. Together, we developed a kind of "time-share" plan in which he would actively schedule his day to include a fair share of play in exchange for sufficient study time. The overall goal was to satisfy both his needs for play and freedom and his desire to graduate law school. He is now doing very well.

Observe, Scrutinize, and Re-focus

For those who seek to be active in their own spiritual growth, the ego can be addressed head-on. And likewise, rather than trying to find a way to better study or escape depression, we can instead discern the extent to which each arising thought is from the ego and for the ego. This disassociated observation of mind gives space for the waters above and in turn grants us access to counter-thoughts based on spiritual values. Three steps are involved: 1) observing the automatic thought; 2) scrutinizing the automatic thought; and 3) focusing on a counter-thought (replacement thought). The following example illustrates these three steps:

1. **Observing the automatic thought:** That driver is such a fool; I'm going to pass him back!

2. **Scrutinizing the automatic thought:** My ego felt slighted because it views driving as a competition and insists on being superior to all other drivers.

3. **Focusing on a counter-thought:** Driving is not a race. It really doesn't matter that he passed me, and I should not take it personally. My goal is to be a safe driver, and patience is a virtue.

Focusing on a single counter-thought may not be enough, though, as the propaganda mill will counter our counter-thoughts with rationalizations and the like:

1. **Observing the automatic thought:** But I have to get to work on time, so I have to go fast!

2. **Scrutinizing the automatic thought:** My ego is constructing this idea that approval from my boss, monetary reward, and the self-satisfaction of doing a "perfect" job are more important than being careful and attentive to the safety of myself and others. My ego is more worried about protecting its own reputation than it is about protecting the lives of others.

3. **Focusing on a counter-thought:** Protecting lives by driving calmly and safely is more important to me than getting to work on time. God, please help me to be patient and calm.

From this newfound place of self-observation, we begin to realize that the ego is always dissatisfied. This realization comes from the waters above. It is a non-ego-based thought that inspires us to look for something better, something higher. **Day 2** ultimately culminates in our coming to fully believe that an ego-based consciousness is fundamentally delusional and that an ego-based lifestyle is inherently harmful. These convictions inspire us to search for a better way of thinking and living, one that is not grounded in the perpetually dissatisfied ego.

Our search for something higher resembles mist rising up from the lower waters to join the higher waters. It may seem as if *we* are searching and growing; but in fact, the Lord is inspiring all that we do in terms of our spiritual growth, as "the attributes of the inner self are . . . the Lord's alone." A ray of spiritual light has shined onto our mind, and we are beginning to get a first taste of the *living water* that the Lord has to offer. Once we have identified the ego as being something inherently disposed to depravity and delusion, we are ready to discover those higher ideas about how to live, such as "love your enemies."

This day is fundamentally about inner observation and discernment. We are gaining a third-person perspective on our own thoughts and emotions. We come to see that there are two basic forms of consciousness: ego-based consciousness and spirit-based consciousness. We see that the latter is light and free like the sky, whereas the former is heavy and tumultuous like the churning sea. The former is brackish, whereas the latter is distilled and pure. We now have the space we need to start making actual decisions.

SUGGESTED PRACTICES

This chapter is about creating a little space so that we can separate from our lower thoughts and adopt a higher, more accurate perspective that leads to healing and a better understanding of life and our own lives.

Cultivating Awareness in Daily Activities

1

During the **Day 2** period, make a point of recognizing the properties and functions of water. Actively appreciate the water that you drink, bathe in, or use to wash things. Spend time contemplating and observing the beauty and grace of water in nature. What parallels come to mind between physical water and the water of the spirit?

2

Spend an entire day actively observing your automatic thoughts. These thoughts are quite often slippery and elusive. A good way to uncover them is to begin by observing your feelings. Sometimes it is easier to recognize our feelings and what we perceive to be their causes than it is to get ahold of our thoughts. When you feel any kind of negativity—hostility, depression, anxiety, excessive desire, frustration, etc.—focus in on what might be giving rise to those feelings. After locating the perceived circumstantial causes, tease out the specific thoughts that accompany those feelings. After identifying our feelings and their apparent causes, we can more easily put into words and give voice to those already existing unconscious thoughts that accompany those feelings.

Meditative Practice

Day 2 is about learning to not identify with our lower thoughts. We begin observing them from a higher perspective and consequently become cognizant of a higher thinking that isn't purely grounded in the delusion of selfhood. During your **Day 0** meditation, you worked to observe with detachment the thoughts that flow through the mind; and you were able to gain insight into how they arise from and serve selfhood. This type of meditation demonstrates perfectly the morning of **Day 2:** separating from our lower thoughts, or the waters below. And during your **Day 1** meditation, you invited the light of God's Word to shine into your mind. This more contemplative practice relates to the evening of **Day 2:** entering into higher thinking, or the waters above.

To succeed at seeing the waters below and in turn at entering the waters above, we must to some degree distance ourselves from both our own thoughts and our own sense of self. If we do not create this distance, then we remain submerged in our lower thoughts and are unable to notice their true illusory nature; and if we become attached to our higher thoughts, the ego will falsely believe that it has created them and in so doing will pollute them, transforming them into lower thoughts within which we become again submerged and blind.

This chapter's meditation, therefore, is a practice that aims to help you gain a sense of mental space and detachment within the expanse of the spiritual dome. By stilling the body and mind, one slowly begins to recognize that their usual activities are not the inherent content of one's being and therefore do not make up one's true selfhood. And when one starts to get in touch with one's being in this way, one begins to feel one's union with all being. And such a taste of one's union is a preview of **Day 7.**

To help establish this state of space, the **Day 2** meditation will be less guided than it will be silent. Before we begin, there is a certain process that I will describe ahead of time, as to do so during the meditation would be disruptive. This particular meditation involves observation from within the dome that surrounds the mind. Thought fragments approach and are observed; but if we give them no attention or even consideration as to what they are about, they fall away. This state is similar to those moments just before falling asleep; here, however, we remain awake and alert. Again, the purpose is to find the space from which we can observe the mind. This space—or dome, as it is described in the verse—is a place of stillness. Your meditation may deepen into a state of non-thought.

During the meditation, I will invite you into this mind space by quoting Psalm 46:10: "Be still, and know that I am God." When you hear these words, simply float within a state of stillness, observing the activity of the mind or entering into a state of non-thought. If the rise and fall of your breathing draws your attention in a way that distracts you from this state of stillness, return to the image of ocean waves that is described in the meditation.

Let's begin with the induction.

[Perform Meditation Induction 2 (p. 59, above)]

Meditation—**Day 2:** Rising above It

From within this meditative state, allow your mind to simply rest upon the rise and fall of the breath.

[Pause for 1 minute]

With each breath in, imagine the ocean waves rising and drawing near to the shore; and with each exhalation, see the gentle waves breaking and sliding up the sand.

[Pause for 1 minute]

Visualize yourself slowly being lifted up above the waves as they continue to rise ... and break ... rise ... and break ... rise ... and break. From up above, look down and see the waves as they swell ... and break below ... swell ... and break below ... swell ... and break below.

From Psalm 46:
"Be still, and know that I am God."

[Pause for 15 seconds]

In the quiet that follows, breathe in and out slowly and deeply.

Doing Practice

Review your experiences and observations from this chapter's meditative practice and daily activities at cultivating awareness. These represent the major themes of the automatic thinking, or propaganda, that runs through your ego-based mind, the waters below. Organize the propaganda into themes (e.g., "external judgments" and "self-judgments"). Then analyze the thoughts within each of these themes, following the three-step observation process discussed on page 84, above. Here are some examples.

	AUTOMATIC THOUGHTS		COUNTER-THOUGHTS
THEME 1: EXTERNAL JUDGMENTS	Observing	Scrutinizing	Focusing on
	I hate life because it sucks.	This perpetuates hostility and causes bad relationships. *Life is not all bad.*	*In this moment, I choose to search for the good in life.*
	Everyone I know is an idiot.	This makes me mean. *Many people I know are kind and intelligent.*	*In this moment, I choose to see the good in this person, even though I feel annoyed.*
	My kids are all messed up. I'm a bad mother.	This makes me mean, and I lose motivation to try. *Though they do have problems, my kids have many good qualities.*	*Francis really throws herself into her sports. Jack takes care of his things. They are trying their best, just like I am. If I was a bad mother, I wouldn't be doing this exercise to improve myself.*

	AUTOMATIC THOUGHTS		COUNTER-THOUGHTS
	Observing	Scrutinizing	Focusing on
THEME 2: SELF-JUDGMENTS	I'm worthless.	This saps my energy and initiative and makes me feel isolated and alone. *I do have value.*	*I'm a valuable human being with many good qualities. I provide for my family and contribute to my company. I'm a faithful husband. I do not need to believe the negative message I received from my parents.*
	I'm a jerk.	This is a negative self-fulfilling prophecy that sinks me into depression and feeds my hostility. *Though I can be hostile, I also show kindness and affection toward others.*	*I'm working to improve, which shows that I want to be a better person. Today, with God's help, will show three people kindness*
	I lost my job, and that means I'm a loser.	This depresses me and causes me to lose motivation. *I may have lost my job, but I'm not a loser.*	*People lose their jobs all the time. I will put my energies into finding a new job and will remain positive about the outlook.*

While these thoughts may seem extreme, they will help clarify how to do this exercise. You may want to sit down with a friend to do this work, as he or she may have a better perspective on the errors in your thinking. Your friend can also help you to come up with positive counter-thoughts. It can be humorous to unearth our irrational thinking with others! If our thinking improves, our behaviors and interactions will also improve.

Suggested Questions for Pondering
and/or Discussion

- What did you learn in your experiences appreciating water? What parallels to spiritual life arose in your mind?

- What was it like to observe your mind throughout the day? How is it different from observing your mind in sitting meditation?

- Were you taken aback by any of your automatic thoughts? Which of them did you find most revealing? Is there anything that you learned about yourself?

- When you began to actively employ new counter-thoughts, did you notice any changes in your behavior? Did you notice any changes in your mood?

- Do you have any further reflections concerning this chapter?

DAY 3: ON SOLID GROUND

And God said, "Let the waters under the sky be gathered together into one place, and let the dry land appear." And it was so. God called the dry land Earth, and the waters that were gathered together he called Seas. And God saw that it was good.

(Genesis 1:9–10)

Translated here as *dry land*, and in other translations as *dry ground*, the Hebrew word *yabbashah* (pronounced *yab-baw-shaw*) actually only means "dry"; the idea of land is implied. An inherent shortcoming of any translation is the inability of the second language to carry all the subtle meanings and associations contained within the mother language. This is an especially difficult problem for translators of ancient Hebrew, a language rich with subtleties, multiple levels of meaning (both symbolic and literal), and interwoven connections between words.

Yabbashah comes from the primary root *yabesh* (pronounced *yaw-bashe*), which means "to be ashamed, confused, or disappointed" or "to fail [at thriving]." These meanings can be understood through the word's symbolic yet more concrete meaning "to dry up," as in the withering of a plant or the drying up of a land in which water is scarce. There is no word in the English language that means at once "drying up," "land," and "humiliation." Including the two times that it appears in this verse, *yabbashah* only appears twelve times throughout the Bible, while the terms *land, ground, earth,* and *dry* appear many hundreds of times in total, using different Hebrew vocabulary. In fact, the word *haaretz,* which is the word typically translated into English as *land,* alone appears more than 1,600 times in the Bible! So we must wonder why this peculiar word, *yabbashah,* was chosen in this context. Maybe this dual meaning was used to describe the land that was appearing out of the seas and in turn was in the process of drying up. *Yabbashah* is used, for example, when the Israelites cross the Red Sea and later the Jordan. This, of course, doesn't diminish the possibility that the Divine Author inspired the earthly scribe to use specific vocabulary for specific connotations. Also, since the idea of land appearing where water had once been would carry a parallel spiritual meaning, it would make sense to use *yabbashah* in order to convey both the literal and the spiritual.

Day 3 deals with a parting in the churning thoughts of the lower mind and gaining a solid foundation, based in humility, for spiritual development. Thus, the word *yabbashah* wonderfully embodies the spiritual meaning conveyed. The people of Israel crossing the Red Sea in order to flee their captors represents something similar: breaking away from our enslavement to the natural mind. Crossing over into the Promised Land after wandering the earth symbolizes moving from a lower state of mind to a higher one. As Swedenborg suggests, the Divine Author is communicating an important message for anyone seeking to understand the parable that is the Bible in its entirety.

While in **Day 2** we were able to enter into the higher thinking of the waters above, in **Day 3** we see that the lower mind fails to function as an adequate framework for living life. So we are experiencing the morning of **Day 3** whenever we look at ourselves and think something like *I am displeased with myself for saying those words; This line of thinking is not productive;* or *I am not proud of these desires that I am having.* Seeing the ugliness of our lower mind instills within us new humility. This newfound humility causes the tempestuous thoughts and desires of the lower mind to *dry up.* And as our faith in the lower mind dries up, we gain a new foundation upon which our future spiritual progress will rest. We stand on the firm, solid determination of our higher thinking in order to reach up toward spiritual ideals. After forming the *dry land,* God calls it *Earth,* translated from a word derived from the same Hebrew word found in the first verse of Genesis, *haaretz,* which means "earth" and "firm." So from a spiritual perspective, I understand this word to mean "firm determination"—a determination that provides us with solid ground for spiritual development.

A Foundation for Growth

Then God said, "Let the earth put forth vegetation: plants yielding seed, and fruit trees of every kind on earth that bear fruit with the seed in it." And it was so. The earth brought forth vegetation: plants yielding seed of every kind, and trees of every kind bearing fruit with the seed in it. And God saw that it was good. And there was evening and there was morning, the third day.

(Genesis 1:11–13)

If the *earth* symbolizes our firm and resolute intention to live for higher things, *vegetation,* which is the product of growth, represents our spiritual development. Despite their incredible beauty, plants are not in the least bit ostentatious; they yield an amazing variety of foods and flavors and are therefore the mainstay of our diet; their flowers are beautiful and fragrant; they clean the air, regulate surface temperature, give out oxygen, bind soil from erosion, and give home to countless numbers of birds and animals. And perhaps most amazing of all, plants feast on sunlight. As warm sunlight nourishes trees, causing them to grow, so God shines onto us and causes us to live. The upward reaching of vegetation to catch the light that streams down from the heavens is a perfect image of human effort to reach up toward God. I recall the words of Jesus: "I am the light of the world" and "In him was life, and the life was the light of all people" (John 8:12; 1:4). The graceful branching nature of plant life even depicts how our thinking works when we are in search of wisdom. And just as vegetable life relies on rain to grow, so this new form of consciousness relies on the higher ideals in the waters above that we entered into in **Day 2.**

In the parable of the sower, Jesus explains that seeds refer to the Word of God. He also tells us that he is the vine and that we are the branches who are to bear fruit (John 15:5). Jesus says that "the tree is known by its fruit" (Matthew 12:33), which means that a person is appreciated by virtue of his or her acts of loving kindness; and a system of ideas is valuable in accordance with its ability to produce good results. It can be clearly understood, then, that the fruit that a tree bears represents actions of service. So when we are eager to reach up toward God, or at least toward higher ideals, our mind is like a fertile field into which God's truth, like seeds, can grow, bringing about deeper and ever-more-expansive understanding and inspiring us to service. These verses from Genesis express a progression—from *seed* to *plants yielding seed* to *fruit with the seed in it* to *fruit trees.* Just as the *seed* represents truth, the upward spiritual striving of **Day 3** initially focuses on knowing God and acquiring spiritual truth.

Our focus on acquiring truth will begin to shape our behaviors, and we will start trying to conform to God's will. Initially, our efforts, like seeds, may feel insignificant and weak; and we find ourselves easily slipping back toward our old self-centered ways. Yet slowly, these efforts build upon one another and become more sturdy and significant until our mind eventually becomes home to fruit trees. Like fruit, our efforts begin to add fragrance and flavor to our lives—little delights of the spirit that sweeten our days. We find gratification in the fact that we were able to hold our tongue when upset or that we were able to remain calm, trusting in God, when faced with a financial downturn. These fruit have within them seeds that promulgate their goodness, as the delight we experience in resisting our anger or in giving our neighbor a helping hand encourages us to do more of the same. This is the stage in which we are reaching up and out to find those higher ideas that will help us become loving. We love truth for the good it produces, so we begin to give of ourselves to other people: spending quality time with our family, volunteering at a soup kitchen, devoting our time to an occupation that benefits society, spending time in devotion, or simply getting ourselves centered so that we don't react from ego.

A teacher of theology at a seminary school once shared an observation with me. He noticed that young pastors focus on truth and morality, whereas older pastors tend to focus more on the Lord's love and mercy. This progression seems to mirror that of our spiritual development.

> We are wholly unaware that [love] is our very life—not just the general life of our whole body and of all our thoughts, but the life of their every least detail. Wise people can grasp this when you ask, "If you take away the effects of love, can you think anything? Can you do anything? As the effects of love lose their warmth, do not thought and speech and action lose theirs as well? Do they not warm up as love warms up?" Still, the grasp of these wise people is not based on the thought that love

is our life, but on their experience that this is how things happen. (*Divine Love and Wisdom* §1)

Moving from a primary focus on truth to a primary focus on love can be seen in the way vegetation grows. In their initial stages, nearly all species reach straight upward (wisdom); but with time, branches form and they begin to reach outward (love). Likewise, as we begin growing in our understanding of God and his will, we begin to reach outward toward others. In so doing, we learn more about God and his ways through our experiences. This learning is represented by the leaves that grow out from the branches, gathering even more light. As the leaves multiply and the plant becomes fuller, so do our good deeds and our ability to refrain from doing harm to others, eventually evolving us into grand and magnificent trees, as we recall from Psalm 1 (pp. 71–72, above). Trees with their silent strength and magnificent beauty are a source of tremendous peace and happiness. Their branches form patterns against the blue sky, as their leaves whisper in the wind and shimmer with sunlight. Trees shelter us with shade and provide generation after generation of children—eyes afresh with wonder and bodies limber and eager for a climb—with a marvelous world to explore.

The Lord evolves our mind into a form that is like a tree planted by the water of life. A person in such a place is capable of comforting others, as if offering them shade when life heats up. Just as a tree's sturdy branches communicate strength and wisdom, such a person can be a safe place for those in need, providing *spiritual* strength and wisdom not so much with words but with mere presence. This kind of person also offers sweet fruits of love and devotion to others.

Each type of tree has a character that mirrors spiritual dispositions. Humor me as I speculate on the "personality" of trees for the sake of illustrating a point. Pines reach straight up toward the sun without as wide a reach as have many deciduous trees. Pines have prickly needles and lack fruit; but they have a wonderful scent, and there is a quiet calm in a pine forest quite unlike that of any other forest. We probably know such "pine-like" people whose focus is on God and who stand morally straight or upright like a pine's trunk. They are perhaps a bit prickly, a little judgmental, and a little less focused on reaching out to others; but they possess a special dignity and wisdom that come with having made efforts at being upright their whole lives. Their thoughts are earnest and spiritual, like the peaceful fragrance of pines. And just as pines tend to grow in groves or as whole forests, such "pine-like" people gather together in church communities of like-minded people. Being amidst their sober approach to life yields a vicarious sobriety, a peace like that found in pine forests.

Then there are the grand-reaching trees. In Nepal, you can find the bodhi tree—also referred to as the peepal tree—under which the Buddha found enlightenment. These trees are truly glorious, with massive gnarly trunks that can grow several meters in circumference and hold up a canopy of large, heart-shaped, emerald-green leaves that shimmer silver when the wind blows. But the most pronounced quality of these trees is their overall shape. Their branches are absolutely massive, reaching out in every direction in wonderful patterns, personifying wisdom and gentle love for all. Bodhis do not stand in clusters but instead can be found all by themselves at the entrances to villages or at the tops of hills. Nepalis often build places beneath these trees since they offer such beautiful shelter. Bodhis may be seen as mirroring people who through spiritual effort have gained wisdom and insight and then use what they have gained to reach out to others in order to offer shade from the heat of life's difficulties.

Fruit trees perhaps represent people who are generous with love and who bless the simple moments of life with sweetness.

While they may lack the far-reaching understanding represented by the grand branches of shade trees, they live life for the sake of nourishing others. There are myriads of tree species and a countless number of individual trees throughout the world. Each of them has its own wonderful qualities, just as each individual possesses unique ways of mirroring the Divine and of blessing others.

One theme undergirding this book is that the parallels between the natural world and the spiritual life of our mind are not coincidental or a contrived analogy; rather, they mirror one another because they are counterparts derived from the same source. For example, God's wisdom and desire to nourish us cause the creation of both physical trees and the spiritual trees evolving within us.

Rooted in the Ego but Growing through Spirit

In **Day 3,** while we may still be grounded in the ego, we are now utilizing it to do good. We discussed the meaning of the newly formed dry land as being a "firm determination" to reach for higher, spiritual ideals. Initially, we believe that this determination is generated by the ego; it is, of course, natural to think that what we decide and what we do are a result of our own volition. But each step of the way, it is God who speaks reality into being.

> The more that angels believe that love and wisdom are within them and claim them for themselves as their own, the more there is nothing angelic within them. To the same extent, then, there is no union with the Lord for them. They are outside the truth; and since truth is identical with heaven's light, they are correspondingly unable to be in heaven. This leads to a denial that they live from the Lord and a belief that they live on their own and therefore that they possess some divine essence. The

life called angelic and human consists of these two elements—freedom and rationality.

This leads to the conclusion that angels have a reciprocal ability for the sake of their union with the Lord, but that the reciprocal element, seen as an ability, is the Lord's and not theirs. As a result, angels fall from angelhood if they abuse this reciprocal element that enables them to feel and sense what is the Lord's as their own by actually claiming it for themselves. . . .

There are people who think that Adam had a kind of freedom or ability to choose that enabled him to love God and be wise on his own, and that this freedom to choose was lost in his descendants. This, however, is wrong. We are not life, but life-receivers . . . and people who are life-receivers cannot love and be wise from their own resources. So when Adam wanted to love and be wise from his own resources, he fell from wisdom and love and was cast out of the garden. (*Divine Love and Wisdom* §§116, 117)

While God is evolving us, our first earnest efforts to reach up toward him and to live a life in line with his own are tied up in the ego. This is important because unless we felt agency, we'd have no feeling of joy; unless we felt personal volition, we'd not make any efforts at all. In this sense, we might understand the earth as representing the ego, as both are necessary environments for the experience of growth: the earth for vegetation and the ego for our spirit.

As God *is* divine selfless love, he must necessarily desire to share joy with us, the *joy* of his selfless love. Paradoxically, to be able to experience this self*less* love, there must be a self to experience it. In other words, we must retain a sense of selfhood in order to experience the joy and peace of God. The sower throws the seeds into the soil, and though the soil nourishes and supports them, the potential for growth and there being a final harvest is latent within the seed itself, not within the earth. We might understand the seed as representing the Word, or truth of God, as both are wherein lies the source of growth. It is the Word alone, and not our ego, that evolves our mind. And the truth of God is that we are loved and that in loving, we are made happy.

In **Day 3** of our spiritual evolution, we wrongly believe that our progress is generated by the self. However, as the following chapters will discuss, the truth is that we only ever act *as if of self.* It is better to act under the false notion of self-generated goodness than it is to stop trying as the result of knowing there is no genuine selfhood. Though our efforts must be rooted in ego, they are nevertheless central to the vitality of our spirit. Just as the pianist has to labor mechanically for many years before she can play effortlessly and with a new sense of spirit, so we must work on moving from a lower state of mind to a higher one before we can live effortlessly within the Spirit of God. We must for some time labor under the sensation and belief that we are the captain of our spiritual journey. Were we prematurely denied this place from which to start, we would lose all motivation and become passive in our efforts. Divine love is the only love; God's effort is the only effort; God's light is the only true light. All of our spiritual evolution rests in God's love alone, but our very existence requires that sense of selfhood that lies at the center of our being. Therefore, until we have an awakening—a vital and moving spiritual encounter with the Divine—we cannot help but mistake all we do as arising from selfhood.

I believe that we can see through the delusion of selfhood only by means of an experience that transcends that selfhood, an experience that by definition must be spiritual. Such spiritual experiences are the subject of **Day 4.** Once a spiritual experience has occurred, our lives will remain rooted in a sense of selfhood, but we will know deep inside that it is only by God's grace and mercy that we are able to live a life of love. We will know that it is not we who bear fruit but that it is God who bears fruit *through* us. He is the vine; we are the branches.

Behavioral Therapy and Its Relationship to the Spiritual

Just as God's hovering over the waters (**Day 1**) parallels Carl Rogers's person-centered therapy, and God's creation of a place that separates the lower waters from the higher waters (**Day 2**) reflects Aaron Beck's cognitive therapy, the emergence of dry land (**Day 3**) can be recognized in a third psychological approach, behavioral therapy.

Behavioral therapy refers to any psychotherapeutic approach that focuses primarily on behavioral change rather than on insights, emotions, or thoughts. A core belief is that behaviors are learned and so can be shaped. Behavioral therapy is broad and includes a diverse range of specific techniques. For example, exposure therapy, in which a person faces their fears with safeguards in place, is an effective form of classical behavioral therapy for treating phobias as well as posttraumatic stress disorder (PTSD). Operant conditioning uses rewards and punishments to effect behavioral change. Role modeling and role playing are very useful for learning anger management, assertiveness, how to overcome anxiety in social situations, and a wide range of other situational needs. Certain types of sitting meditation can be considered a form of behavioral therapy in that during meditation, one is controlling behavior to effect a mental and emotional change.

Forgiveness

In recent years, some spiritual tools have proven so fruitful that they are making inroads even into behavioral therapy, garnering support from the scientific and scholarly community.

Forgiveness, which is a spiritual act of selfless love, is a good example. Forgiving others has wonderful psychological effects, while failing to do so (holding a grudge) causes our most harmful, painful, and offensive past experiences to stay with us in the perpetual present.

Stanley, who was a client of mine, was abused by a bully in school. Ten years after this had occurred, Stanley dreaded any building that reminded him of his school and experienced flashbacks and nightmares related to what had happened. He had all the symptoms of PTSD. According to current official diagnostic criteria, this diagnosis can only be given if the trauma involved real or perceived *severe* bodily harm to one's self or another; but in my practice, I have often worked with victims of school bullying who exhibit all the symptoms of PTSD. Initially, I attempted to help him by using a range of exposure therapies, which rank among the most successful known therapies for PTSD and other anxiety disorders. Exposure is a form of behavioral therapy that entails helping the client face his or her fears related to the past, present, and future. By exposing them little by little to the source of irrational anxiety, the client learns that they can experience the memory or other trigger without danger. This technique, however, produced only mild relief for Stanley. In a later session, he confessed to often ruminating about murdering the bully and disposing of his body in grotesque ways. I told him that resentment is like stepping in dog dirt and then rather than moving on, taking off your shoe and putting it in your backpack to focus on it again later. Happiness simply cannot coexist with hate. With a little coaxing, Stanley was able to forgive the bully, and he achieved wonderful results. He is no longer plagued by nightmares and flashbacks; once constant, his feelings of stress and depression have become intermittent; and he no longer has murderous feelings.

Meditation

Meditation is another spiritual practice that is becoming very popular in secular behavioral psychology. I believe meditation to be the single most valuable psychological practice available, and there isn't one client of mine who hasn't heard my spiel on meditation and its benefits or received my encouragement to give it a try. Primarily used as a way of detaching consciousness from automatic thinking, meditation is an outstanding practice to promote **Day 2** growth. Having gained some perspective over our lower thinking, meditation can also be an active way of reaching upward toward God in search of higher, more spiritual forms of consciousness. A growing volume of empirical evidence shows meditation to produce tremendous positive effects on many axes of mental health, including attention span, tranquility, happiness, empathy, and resilience in the face of emotional and physical discomfort. Brain imaging shows that meditation increases the connections between various parts of the brain and also alters how the brain functions. For these reasons, meditation not only helps us to recognize and rise above the waters below, but it also causes us to become better people, the stuff of **Day 3**. With the help of guided meditation in conjunction with other therapies, several clients have been able to move beyond crippling phobias; a number of them have been able to work through deep pain; one young client was able to improve her behaviors so that they were no longer disruptive; and another was able to reduce a constant low-level anger that followed her through her days.

One client of mine suffered from severe anxiety, obsessive thoughts, and deep depression, but she was not showing significant improvement from therapy. This client would come for a session, and we'd look at all the evidence that indicated— even proved—that her fears were unfounded. This was good, solid cognitive therapy (**Day 2**), and by the end of the session, she'd feel better and see more rationally. Invariably, when she returned the following week, though, she'd be fully convinced that her fears were based in reality. She would say that she felt good for a day after each of our sessions but then slipped back to where she was before. I constantly encouraged her to start meditation. In fact, a number of our sessions involved leading her through guided meditation. She eventually began to meditate on her own every morning, and she soon noticed improvements. She gained insight into the fact that her fears were unrealistic, she became more productive, and she felt happier.

Mindfulness

Mindfulness is a third spiritual practice that dovetails with behavioral therapy; it entails focusing on the here and now rather than on the squall of upset that comes along with the past and future concerns of the ego-based mind. By itself, it is a good technique for helping us gain some mental space from the ego-based thoughts of the waters below. Supplementing mindfulness with a seemingly minor element, though, transforms this practice into a wonderful way to reach up toward God in support of our **Day 3** efforts. Rather than focusing on the here and now with a sort of empty, non-judgmental focus—the secular form of mindfulness—we can focus on the present as a revelation of the immediate presence of God within the here and now. I have found that this practice can effectively usher in a palpable, powerful perception of the Lord's loving presence within all things and all moments.

I believe that other forms of spiritual practice will eventually make their way into the field of psychological counseling. For example, the selfless giving of one's time and material possessions to those in need creates a deep sense of happiness, contentment, and purpose. Just as important as forgiving others is the act of asking for their forgiveness; by apologizing to others, we make it easier for them to forgive us, and we receive the tranquility of having done our part to make peace. Perhaps, one day, therapists will more seriously and significantly discuss the idea of the delusion of selfhood, and they will advocate specific practices that help their clients escape that delusion.

Rewards and Punishments

Even seemingly non-spiritual forms of behavioral counseling can promote spiritual goals. Behavioral therapists often employ positive consequences to strengthen positive behaviors and negative consequences to "extinguish" negative behaviors. Since this approach is more or less identical with the kind used by animal trainers, I initially felt disdain toward behavioral therapy. However, I watched one young client of Dr. Arun Kunwar, my supervisor, evolve from a baseline of screaming and physically abusive hatred to a boy who no longer exhibited violence and who was able to employ a vocabulary that extended beyond his previous obscenities. It's truly amazing how mundane motivators can lead to moral improvement.

Using rewards and punishments, one client of mine learned how to follow classroom expectations and developed better social skills. In a behavioral therapy-based diet program developed by Dr. Kunwar and myself, many people whose previous attempts at losing weight were unsuccessful were finally able to slim down. These are not grand spiritual achievements, but behavioral therapy succeeds in helping people function better amidst the details of living, and the devil is in the details. Spirituality is neither a head game nor something only of the heart; it is ultimately in the *hands,* the doing. If we attempt to work on our spiritual life while neglecting to take care of the important mundane things, such as keeping a tidy room, we are missing a part of the big picture.

Day 3 is made of effort and change, which is to say that it consists of a lot of hard, plodding work. We can set ourselves spiritual goals and use earthly motivators to help ourselves along. In fact, to be unwilling to use low-level motivators for spiritual ends may be a product of the ever-deceptive conceit of the ego, that part of us that does not actually want to change. The Lord's main tools in shepherding the Israelites through the wilderness and into the Promised Land were rewards and punishments, carrot and stick. Just as trees draw up nutrients and water from the soil while reaching up toward the sky, so we must use earthly, mundane means to achieve spiritual goals.

My favorite experience using behavioral therapy involved an entire family that was out of control and falling apart. The children were insolent and disobedient; the mother often slapped them (something not too rare and not considered child abuse in Nepal). The father was grumpy and disengaged, except when barking out criticisms of his wife and children. Despite these obvious problems, it was also clear that they loved each other. I taught the mother how to create and use a behavior chart in which the daily duties of the children were written, and I suggested to her that she post it on the wall where everyone could see it. If her children performed a particular duty, she would check the box next to that duty. After a week of keeping track of their progress, the mother would give them either a reward or a punishment based on their performance. If they were rude, violent, or disobedient, then they would lose phone, computer, and television privileges. Over the course of therapy, this family made great progress. It was wonderful to watch how the love that was buried under chaos was able to bloom as that chaos was resolved. Both the children and the parents had to do some hard work. Behavioral techniques helped them along toward a goal they all wanted but couldn't before achieve—a happier family. Mundane methods produced spiritual results.

Role Playing

Role playing is another behavioral method and is often used to overcome anger issues. After identifying antecedents to the outburst, we then brainstorm a number of healthy alternative responses from which the client can choose what seems best for them. Finally, we role play the problematic situations so that they can practice their newly chosen responses. Overcoming rage is clearly spiritual progress.

Behavioral therapy produces change by focusing not on insights or on thought patterns but instead on the changing of overt behaviors through such means as positive and negative consequences, repeated practice, and mentoring. It can be as simple as making ourselves write down a gratitude list each day or even forcing ourselves to smile. The most difficult time of my life was when I first moved to Nepal. I was simultaneously carrying the burden of culture shock, being a new father to eleven beautiful but wounded children, learning how to manage the staff of our nonprofit organization, working on the legal and logistical elements of the orphanage, and figuring out how to function in a cross-cultural marriage. There were also many other massive stresses, such as crooked landlords, treacherous board members, and loved ones having to endure impossible situations. In addition to facing all of these challenges, I had left everything I knew and loved back in the United States, and I felt alone, with very little support or sense of comfort as I tried to navigate my new world.

During those first few shattering years in Nepal, forcing myself to smile made a huge difference in my mood. I also forced myself to laugh each day. Most of the time, my forced smiles and laughter led to genuine smiles and laughter because the non-spontaneity felt so silly. Here again we have earthly means to spiritual goals. I have since read studies showing that forcing smiles and laughter does indeed lift mood.

We often think that what we believe and what we value shape what we do. While this is true, it is equally true that what we *do* becomes what we believe and what we value. If we force ourselves to smile, we feel happy. If we force ourselves to keep a clean house, we come to appreciate keeping our house clean and learn to enjoy the process of cleaning. If we force ourselves to breathe slowly and deeply, we find that our mind becomes calmer. If we force ourselves to do the works of love, such as holding our tongue, serving others, and doing kind things, we begin to feel love.

> The act comes first; our will to do it comes after. What we do at the beck of intellect we eventually do with a will and finally take on as a habit. At that point it is infused into our inner, rational self. Once it has been infused we no longer do good from truth but from good, because we start to feel a certain bliss and to sense something of heaven in it. This feeling remains with us after death, and through it the Lord lifts us into heaven. (*Secrets of Heaven* §4353:3)

Once we begin working toward acts of selfless love, they take hold of us, planting seeds, sending out roots, bearing fruit, and then multiplying in our lives until eventually filling our consciousness and becoming second nature. **Day 3** is the first day to feature living organisms (*vegetation*) as part of God's "good" work. During **Days 1** and **2,** we were gaining distance from spiritual death and delusion; in **Day 3,** however, we are actually reaching toward and gaining spiritual life.

SUGGESTED PRACTICES

This chapter is about the newly given humility from which we take what we know and put it into practice in an effort to reach up toward the Lord and out to serve others.

Cultivating Awareness in Daily Activities

1

The nice thing about mindfulness is that we can do it at any time. By focusing on the here and now, we can create space enough to attune not only to what is around us but also to the perfect love that is the Lord's ever-presence. This is Lord-centered mindfulness, wherein God is not merely a thought or image in the mind but is a felt experience in the depths of the spirit. During the **Day 3** period, make efforts at this practice of Lord-centered mindfulness.

2

Nature serves us well as a window into our own spiritual qualities. Reflect, for example, on your favorite species of tree. Consider its most attractive qualities, and then notice how they translate into qualities of the spiritual realm (e.g., strength, gracefulness, peace, devotion to the Lord, or generosity). After giving some time to contemplating these qualities, generate three concrete things you can do during your day to better embody them. Also, come up with three specific thought patterns or internal behaviors that will move you even closer to embodying these admirable spiritual qualities.

Meditative Practice

Day 3 is about reaching up from a state of humility toward God and toward higher spiritual truths in order to make behavioral improvements in our natural lives. It is about digging our roots down into our sense of self-based determination so that we grow strong and healthy in these changes. The ultimate goal is to begin bearing the fruit of love and goodwill for others. This meditation includes prayers, a visualization, and quotes from both the Bible and the writings of Swedenborg. The prayers are an invitation to humility before God; the visualization is an effort to connect our spirit to that of God, which is revealed and embodied as a tree, the tree of life; and the quotes are God's vitalizing light. This is an invitation to reach up to the leaves of our mind and receive God's wisdom and love so that we can bear fruit in our lives.

Let's begin with the induction.

[Perform Meditation Induction 2 (p. 59, above)]

Meditation—**Day 3:** On Solid Ground

From within this meditative state, listen to the following prayer and let it fill your mind: "Lord, I humble myself before you. Without you, I am nothing and without meaning. I surrender my life to you and thank you for each breath . . . for each heartbeat."

[Pause for 20 seconds]

"Lord, please accept my prayer and accept my life into your hands—to create in me a new heart of love and humility and a life of dedication to you."

[Pause for 30 seconds]

Now, imagine a beautiful tree that reaches up for the light of the sun, its emerald leaves shimmering in the golden glow. See the texture of the bark on the strong trunk and the base of the tree where the roots stretch down, anchoring it. See its fruits.

[Pause for 30 seconds]

Allow yourself to be filled with gratitude for this tree, this representation of life itself. Think about the different parts of the tree, allowing yourself to unite with them in gratitude.

[Pause for 45 seconds]

Now, enter into the very life of this tree, reaching up with your mind to know the Lord and deeper spiritual truth. As leaves catch the light of the sun, your mind reaches to catch the light of God's truth. Your roots reach down to connect your natural life to the higher reaches of your spiritual mind, to goodwill and an awareness of the Lord. The fruits of your labor are the crown of this life.

[Pause for 1 minute; then read the following]

From Jeremiah 17:
Blessed are those who trust in the Lord, whose trust is the Lord. They shall be like a tree planted by water, sending out its roots by the stream. It shall not fear when heat comes, and its leaves shall stay green; in the year of drought it is not anxious, and it does not cease to bear fruit.

[Pause for 30 seconds]

From Ezekiel 47:
On the banks, on both sides of the river, there will grow all kinds of trees for food. Their leaves will not wither nor their fruit fail, but they will bear fresh fruit every month, because the water for them flows from the sanctuary. Their fruit will be for food, and their leaves for healing.

[Pause for 30 seconds]

From Secrets of Heaven *§885:*
The tree stands for the people of a church that embodies the Lord's kingdom. The fruit stands for the good that results from love and charity, and the leaf, for the truth that develops out of it. That truth is used for the instruction and regeneration of the human race, which is why the leaf is said to serve as medicine.

[Pause for 30 seconds]

From Coronis *§29:*
No one can ascend to the ... spiritual mind, unless [they] eat of the trees of life in the garden of God. For by eating of these a [person] is enlightened and made whole, and conceives

faith; and through the nourishment of their fruits [a person]
acquires the conviction that all good is from the Lord, who is
the tree of life, and not the smallest portion from [them]; and
yet by abiding together and operating together, hence by the
Lord's being in [them] and [they] in the Lord, [they] must
do good of [themselves], but still be in the belief and confi-
dence that it is not from [themselves] but from the Lord.

If [they] believe otherwise, [they do] what appears like
good, in which there is evil inwardly, because there is merit;
and this is eating of the trees of the knowledge of good and
evil, among which dwells the serpent.

[Pause for 90 seconds]

ooooo

In the quiet that follows, allow yourself to meditate
deeply on these passages. Catch the light of their truth with
the leaves of your spirit. What will you do to bring these
truths to fruition in your life?

Doing Practice

1

As discussed at the opening of this chapter, humility is the
foundation for progress in **Day 3**. Spend time in humble devotion to God. You may want to take five to fifteen minutes every
morning for devotional reading, followed by prayer for humility and for God to fill your words and actions with his love.

2

Just as trees bear fruit, try to bear some form of fruit that will
help nourish the lives of others. You may wish to serve or do
something kind for someone. Try to avoid hoping for anything
in return; such hopes are only a product of the ego. One way

to work on managing the ego is to do your act of kindness in secret.

3

If you are holding any resentment toward someone, try forgiving them, remembering what it would be like to have to carry that filthy, smelly shoe around in your backpack all day. Write them a letter, explaining how they hurt you and the consequences that their actions have had in your life. Let them know that you forgive them.

4

Think of some aspect of your life about which you would like to make improvements. Take a few minutes to give some serious consideration to your thoughts and feelings on this matter. Then, write down on a piece of paper all the *external* factors that influence this part of your life. Knowing these factors will help give you some idea about when and in what specific ways you are triggered by circumstance and most likely in need of help. Now consider and make note of the *internal* factors that drive you to perform this act. For example, if you lash out in anger, you may find that it is caused by a sense of urgency or a feeling of being rushed, which may in turn be caused by your prioritizing the details of your day-to-day schedule over having trust in the Lord and maintaining harmony with others. After taking some time to ponder the external and internal factors that contribute to your behavior, come up with some concrete steps that you can take to effect the desired change. Make a plan that describes how you will act out these concrete steps on a daily basis, taking into consideration when, where, and with whom you will do so. Reward yourself when you fulfill your tasks, and deprive yourself when you do not. Depriving ourselves some little daily luxury can be very effective in reminding us of our goals—we are enlisting material means to support spiritual goals. Include any other important information about how to implement your plan—the more concrete, the better. Record your progress.

Suggested Questions for Pondering and/or Discussion

- Do you know anyone who has put a lot of effort into knowing the Lord, moving away from selfishness, and living a life of service to others in some way? How do you feel about this person? Have you seen firsthand the results of their efforts? What do they say about how their lives have changed after putting in so much effort? If they were a tree or plant, how would you describe them?

- What was it like to practice Lord-centered mindfulness? What would you say are its advantages or disadvantages when compared to the more attenuated, secular form of mindfulness that opens the doorway to becoming present?

- What were the qualities you found most attractive in your tree of choice? What was your experience of working to better embody those characteristics?

- Did any of the readings in the meditation hold a special meaning for you? If so, which one, and why? Did any of them cause an emotional or spiritual reaction you weren't expecting?

- With the forgiveness task, were you able to decide to let go of your resentment toward someone? If so, was it hard to do? How did you feel before and afterward?

- Did you engage with the practice of making a concrete plan to improve some part of your life? What was the plan? How did it go in practice? What was the result?

- Do you have any further reflections concerning this chapter?

DAY 4: ENCOUNTERING GOD

And God said, "Let there be lights in the dome of the sky to separate the day from the night; and let them be for signs and for seasons and for days and years, and let them be lights in the dome of the sky to give light upon the earth." And it was so. God made the two great lights—the greater light to rule the day and the lesser light to rule the night—and the stars. God set them in the dome of the sky to give light upon the earth, to rule over the day and over the night, and to separate the light from the darkness. And God saw that it was good. And there was evening and there was morning, the fourth day.

(Genesis 1:14–19)

It was a spark of sunlight on a spot of mica that transported Martin Buber (1878–1965) into the state of mystical oneness that inspired his famous work *I and Thou*. The underlying theme of his book is the importance of having these unitive experiences. Rather than perceiving things as outside and separate from ourselves, deepest truth is known, he argues, in what he calls the "I-Thou" encounter—perception of unity with what is usually perceived as other than ourselves. The resulting gestalt of observer and observed is a higher reality than either of the two components on its own or even than the mere addition of one to the other. In that moment, Buber became absorbed with the sunlit mica in such a way that he no longer comprehended a division between himself and the object. He goes on to say that such experiences are actually mystical unions and that they can occur not only with what is around us but also with God.

Whether they are dramatic or subtle, such moments of mystical awakening and their after-effects are, as I see it, the substance of **Day 4**. **Day 4** is when our spirit first becomes receptive to the tremendous warmth and brilliance of firsthand experience with an interactive, perceptible Lord. No longer is God a mere mental construction, something distant or ephemeral; he is now a living, human God with whom we have a genuine relationship.

> If we do not think of God as being in a human form, we can have no definite idea of God, because what is incomprehensible does not take shape in the mind. . . .
>
> The Lord is the only true human being, and we become human only if we become receptive to what is divine from him. (*New Jerusalem* §§305:3, 307:2)

It is the difference between diffuse light obscured by clouds and the clear, unobstructed rays of the shining sun. From here onward, our spiritual life is no longer governed primarily by doctrine or faith; it is guided by love. Our life is imbued with the realization that the perfect love of the Lord is always immediately present with us.

This can be a difficult transition for many people—shifting from an abstract, more generalized relationship with God to a personal relationship with the living Lord; for one thing, such a relationship requires having a deep and abiding faith in the personhood of God. It is one thing to believe that there is a divine force and quite another to believe in Jesus as the one and only God or even to believe that the God of the universe is best understood as human. Another challenge is that believing in God as human can make him much more present and personal, and this can be threatening to our selfish ways.

My Journey with God

Once I became willing to believe that God existed, which was during my sophomore year in college, I wanted to know more about God. Who was God? What was God? After having studied and gained from a variety of other philosophies and traditions, I decided to find out more about Jesus and his claim to being God. Not wanting to pin my faith on miracles, I opened a copy of the Bible, reading only those words from the four Gospels that are recorded as what Jesus uttered. I was moved.

It was so clear that Jesus's whole life and teachings were devoted to one thing: selfless love. He didn't care about ritualism, rule, or even moralism, except to the extent that these things were used as the foundation of our true peace and happiness. Jesus's command is quite simply that we love one another, "that [our] joy may be complete" (John 15:11). Sharing and encouraging selfless love for the sake of the well-being of humanity was and is his sole purpose. Jesus identified himself as God, which was a difficult claim for me not only to accept but also to dismiss given the truth and goodness of his other statements. As C. S. Lewis noted, Jesus presents us with a trilemma: he is either a liar or a lunatic or indeed God. I couldn't believe that someone so focused on love could be a liar, and nothing I read about him indicated insanity.

So, on a philosophical level, I began to ponder the idea that Jesus might be God—or rather, the possibility that the Creator of the universe might have actually incarnated on our tiny earth. Initially, this seemed impossibly ludicrous. The more I thought about it, though, the more it seemed likely, even inevitable: if God truly is pure love, then God would not only *want* to communicate love to us, but he would *have* to communicate his love. Our existence and the wondrous beauty of creation are surely communications of God's love, but is it enough to satisfy divine love's need to communicate itself, especially if our ability to sense these things as gifts of that love was waning? Would a loving father be content with sending his children gifts via postal mail, or would he demand to be with his children in person so that they know not just the gifts but also the sender? And more than that, would he not want to have a reciprocal relationship with his beloved children?

I was unable to think of a convincing motive for the early church to either invent a Messiah or alter the message they had heard from the person whom they believed to be a Messiah. Ultimately, I became willing to submit—as best I could—my life to Jesus as the face and hands of a loving God. I could not (and still cannot) think of any greater purpose to which I would be willing to dedicate my life—to make my God. The fact that faith in Jesus has made me a better person also helps me to believe that he is God.

That there is one God who is human is also revealed in what is considered the pinnacle Hindu text, the *Bhagavad Gita,* wherein Krishna reveals to Arjuna that he, God, is best known in human form, not as a cosmic force, and that though people worship many gods, there is in fact only one God who will incarnate. The *Bhagavad Gita* explains very clearly the situation of the illusion of selfhood, which I will discuss later in this chapter. In this account of Krishna, the human manifestation of the one and only God explains to Arjuna, an archer who is not eager to enter battle, that though he must enter the battlefield and fight, he must understand that he has already won the battle from eternity and that it is he alone who fights. Many highlight what is different between Christianity and other traditions, but as an avid seeker of spiritual truth, I can't help but see many parallels. Long before Jesus, seekers from an entirely different culture arrived at an understanding of God's nature. In both cases, the message is, "Search, and you will find" (Matthew 7:7).

When thinking about the mystical experience of oneness, it is perhaps common to depersonalize the Divine; in that experience, God becomes a nebulous miasma of cosmic energy. For oneness, there must also be otherness, or twoness. Love is what binds the two together. Jesus describes the relationship between himself and those who abide in him as that of vine and branches—two distinct elements bound together as one.

The powerful experience of oneness supersedes our typical vision of reality based on division, a vision of reality that arises from within the delusion of self. When such an experience of oneness has been had, the mind knows that oneness is the ultimate and irrefutable truth, regardless of the "proofs" offered by our five senses or by the sciences constructed upon them. Divine love is complemented by divine wisdom.

> There is one human God who is the source of everything. All the elements of human reason unite in, and in a sense center on, . . . the oneness of God. . . .
>
> The true divine essence is love and wisdom. If you gather together everything you know, focus your mind's insight on it, and look through it carefully from some spiritual height to discover what is common to everything, the only conclusion you can draw is that it is love and wisdom. These two are essential to every aspect of our life. (*Divine Love and Wisdom* §§23, 28)

The Dawning of the Sun

Day 4 brings to us the profound realization that the self is not only unreliable but that it is of itself nonexistent, just as a branch cannot of itself exist but exists only as a vessel for the life of the tree or vine from which it grows. The Lord, by his will alone, is evolving us. We cannot have faith, except for the grace of the Lord. We cannot have any motivation toward higher things, except for the mercy of the Lord. We cannot say a single true word or perform a single good deed, except for the fact that the Lord is forever flowing into our lives. In other words, our humanness is not our own; it is God working within us. When this fact sinks down deep into the heart and spirit, we for the first time genuinely encounter the Lord in a living way and experience the oneness that is his life within us.

As do many mystics, Swedenborg states clearly in a number of ways that selfhood is illusory. Throughout his works, he refers to working *as if of self* while knowing that God is in fact the doer.

> [It is a] law of divine providence . . . that we should act in freedom and in accord with reason . . . and [a law of divine providence] that we should do this for ourselves, even though it is being done by the Lord—that is, in apparent autonomy. (*Divine Providence* §129)

Despite our lack of selfhood, we must still act as if we are doing so from ourselves, since participating in this way is the means by which the Lord effects salvation.

> Everyone in the heavens knows, believes, and even perceives that nothing good is intended and done by the self and that nothing true is thought and believed by the self. Everything comes from the Divine, which means from the Lord. Anything good and true from the self is not good or true, because there is no life from the Divine within it. (*Heaven and Hell* §8)

We read in Malachi 4:2 that "the sun of righteousness shall rise, with healing in its wings." This is a clear prophecy of Jesus as "Emmanuel," which means "God is with us" (Matthew 1:23). Just as all the light and warmth supporting life on earth radiate from the natural sun, all truth and love sustaining the life of our spirit shine out from the Lord, who is symbolized by the spiritual sun.

> [The spiritual] sun is not God. Rather, it is an emanation from the divine love and wisdom of the Divine-Human One. The same is true of warmth and light from that sun. "The sun that angels see" . . . does not mean the Lord himself. It means that first emanation from him that is the highest form of spiritual warmth. (*Divine Love and Wisdom* §93)

It is no coincidence that the sun and the moon do not appear in the Creation sequence until after the vegetable kingdom has been established upon the earth. This explains our spiritual evolution precisely. It is not that the sun, moon, and stars did not previously exist; it is that the higher things of our mind were still obscured by the delusion of selfhood. God has always been and always will be immediately with us. As the seeds of truth are planted within us, vegetation represents what comes of our efforts to think well, to live well, and to will well. We attempt to do what is right and what is loving from a sense of self-determination, and these self-based efforts of **Day 3** come first so that our sense of self is not shattered too suddenly. An instant transition from faith in self to total awareness of the Lord as the sole source of our very life would evaporate our sense of meaning and joy. Our initial self-based efforts toward spiritual living are a means of weaning us away from faith in self; they provide us with a way to slowly and mercifully purify our consciousness from its delusion of self-life.

When from a belief in self as doer we work to live a spiritual life, we increasingly gain spiritual wisdom in a number of ways. Such wisdom begins with the recognition of our weaknesses and inherent limitations. Despite our most sincere and concerted efforts, we are never able to reach the goal of a truly spiritual life. Some of our thoughts remain base and some of our actions remain selfish. We keep working, but we keep failing. After years of such toil, like Jacob slaving away for Laban (a Hebrew name that means "white," which symbolizes purity) in Genesis 29–30, we find that we can never satisfy this desire for purity. So we give up. We give up on self. Chronic failure and despair prepare us to really let the Lord into our lives in a much more profound and personal way than we had at first imagined.

The realization that we are not very good at loving others or at refraining from our selfish ways also helps us forgive others for their weaknesses. We become less judgmental, and our attempts at showing love allow actual selfless love from the Lord to flow in. It is as if we are creating vessels that are fit for receiving life. As a result, our view of reality rises above the merely material view. The branches of the trees receive light from above and so the tree that is our wisdom grows stronger and higher. As our wisdom matures, a more transcendent and universal vision of reality begins to replace our egocentric view.

As our sense of unity with others develops, we become more empathetic, devoting our time and energy toward bettering and blessing their lives. Love increasingly flows into and through our lives. As this occurs, we begin to understand that love is a much more awesome power and motivation than anything we can generate from our own sense of selfhood. Love is higher than our personhood, as it is a universal reality that is given and shared in common among all people. In other words, we awaken to the fact that there is only one love and that we are all made one in that love. This is the dawning of **Day 4,** which flows naturally from the work of **Day 3.**

In my senior year of undergraduate school, I had what to this day remains the most profound and life-altering experience of my life. It began with a visceral sensation that underneath all the suffering and trials, life is guided by the unseen providence of the Lord's love, leading all things to an ultimate destination of pure love and goodness. This sensation was wedded to an expansive joy and excitement that grew out of my being released from twenty years of obsessive worry over the suffering of human beings on earth and over the doctrine of eternal hell, which is another form of human suffering. With liberation from this lifelong burden came an abiding sense of God's palpable presence and love permeating all of reality. Day by day the scope and intensity of my experience grew. From my innermost being, I knew without any doubt that all of life was a part of the divine oneness. Being a part of this oneness, I sensed the undeniable truth that its reality is ordained by divine love, ordered by divine wisdom, and guided by perfect divine providence. I felt a sacred current running in and through everything, ushering us forward toward a destiny of unimaginable goodness. Everything shone with God's presence and love. At that time, when I read the Word of God, I had a very strong experience of its profound power—that it was somehow simultaneously describing the life of my spirit and creating that life in that precise moment. It was very overwhelming. I also felt a sense of unity with others. The social masks that divide us dropped away, and I was able to deeply feel their secret inner pains and joys. Due to the oneness I felt with others and with all of life, my sense of self was smashed.

A firsthand encounter with God need not be so shattering or dramatic. The process of spiritual evolution is uniquely beautiful within each individual. It may be obvious or hidden; it may be sudden or gradual. It might manifest as a blossoming sensation and appreciation of God's presence in others, in Scripture, within nature, or within the here and now. It might come as a dream or as a warm peace that permeates one's being. No one process is better than another, because within all of these variations, there is only one way—the way of God.

We Are Vessels for the Lord

Encountering the Lord causes faith in selfhood to melt like ice exposed to the rising of a warm, spring sun.

> The inflow of life from God brings these delights [of love] and pleasures [of wisdom] with it, like an inflow of springtime light and warmth into human minds, into all kinds of birds and animals, even into plants, which then sprout and grow. For love's delights and wisdom's pleasures open up spirits and make them fit to receive, the way joy and happiness open up faces and make them fit for the inflow of the soul's gaiety. (*Soul-Body Interaction* §13)

We have come to see that we are not the doer; we are vessels for what is being done by the true doer, the Lord. He is the potter, and we are the clay. He is the vine, and we are the branches. While the *delusion* of selfhood can be weakened or even destroyed, the *illusion* that we are willing, choosing, and doing from our selfhood remains. Though we experience life from within a sense of selfhood and feel as if we make decisions and take actions, we break through the delusion when we no longer believe that this sense of autonomy is true.

The illusion of selfhood is one of the most precious gifts that God endows us, and it will never be taken away; only from within this illusion are we able to have relationship with others and with God. We can comprehend oneness only from within the plurality of individualities. We can know love only from within a sense of separation, a sense of selfhood.

The illusion of separate being—selfhood—afforded by a consciousness bound within space-time is required for love to exist. It is amazing that something so exalted as love is sustained by something as potentially destructive and false as illusion. Swedenborg often writes that heaven and hell are both required to sustain human freedom.

Freedom comes from the equilibrium between heaven and hell; if we did not have this freedom we could not be reformed. (*New Jerusalem* §149)

If the ultimate truth were seen—that the I AM alone is—separate consciousness would cease to exist; and without otherness, love would cease to have any meaning, and the I AM would be as nothingness. In this way, God makes himself one with creation. For years, I thought it very odd that the Nepali word *maya* means both "illusion" and "love." However, when more recently I saw that love exists only when sustained by the illusion of separate beings and individual consciousness, it made sense.

Just how priceless and important this illusion is can be seen in what is permitted to sustain its existence. The cost of the illusion of selfhood is all evil and sin. The deluded ego harms others in its efforts to both obtain what it desires and protect itself. Despite the evil that arises, the suffering that comes with a sense of selfhood is an acceptable tradeoff for an eternity of bliss, a bliss that is possible only when there is a sense of self. If it were not acceptable, then there would not be evil. Divine, selfless love by its very nature cannot help but give of itself to others. The entire universe is the expression of divine love, created so that sentient beings might experience the eternal joy that is divine love.

The Moon and Stars

The sense of God's immediate presence does not remain with unwavering intensity; it rises and sets in cycles—*for seasons and for days and years,* as it says in Genesis 1:14. Though the warmth and brilliance of the Lord's presence fades to evening and then to night, our memory of the experience sustains us through the darkness. This memory is the moon that reflects the light of the sun, thereby illuminating the nighttime of our spirit. The darkness we feel is never as complete as it was before. When I don't feel close to the Lord, I still have faith in his presence—a faith that is based in having had firsthand experience.

> The light of the moon is the faith that results from caring, and the light of the sun is the intelligence that then follows from love, which is given us by the Lord. (*Revelation Unveiled* §53:2)

When the sun is out, we see clearly. Similarly, when we are warmed by the sensation of the Lord's presence, we see life clearly. Under the light of the moon, we can see our way around well enough, though we might occasionally stumble. Similarly, when we are not operating from an immediate sense of the Lord's life within us but instead from only our faith in the Lord, our experience of life isn't as clear and vibrant. We can travel the spiritual path reasonably well, but we might occasionally fall away from it. Sometimes, even the moon disappears—our faith wanes until we begin to doubt God in some manner.

This happened to me after experiencing a terrible earthquake (7.9 on the Richter scale) that devastated much of Nepal. Nine thousand people died. We went out into the villages every day to provide food and materials for temporary shelters for those in need. Village after village was razed to the ground. One valley, in particular, looked as though a giant had stomped on each and every hamlet and home. I noticed afterward that I didn't feel close to God; in fact, I had no interest in God whatsoever. Just like that, spirituality and my relationship with Jesus seemed irrelevant to my life. It's not that I doubted God's existence; it was simply that my relationship with him was no longer of any importance. I had never felt that way before. Initially, I supposed it to be a result of my hyper-focus on the relief work I was doing in the wake of the earthquake—getting done what needed to be done on a very practical level. But after the work was finished, I still had no interest in approaching God. It was almost two months later that I began to realize I was feeling angry at God. Intellectually, I was able to cope with what had happened; I still trusted that God was leading all to good. This intellectual trust is probably why it took me so long to clue in to the fact that having seen so much death and destruction, my heart was grieving and in deep despair. My heart was upset with God. It was a dark night of the soul.

At the time, I was forced to delve into the Gospel of Matthew in order to prepare for a course that I was about to teach. Revisiting the Word of the Lord ushered in the return of the sun into my spirit. By his Word, the Lord reached out and met me, and that somehow allowed all the pent-up grief to begin pouring out. The parables, teachings, and stories in the Gospel of Matthew came together and guided me back to morning, just as the stars guide a sailor through the night.

The stars of the spirit are facts and ideas about God and life. They are distant from our heart and so cold. They do not shine brilliantly, but they hold position reliably and can be assembled into meaning. The wise men from the East followed a star until they were face to face with God. In the same way, if we earnestly search for higher truth, we begin to map patterns and assemble ideas into constellations that make sense and in turn begin to guide our thoughts. The pursuit of spiritual wisdom makes one able to assemble natural, scientific facts in a way that makes them shine with spiritual truth. It also makes one able to assemble meaning out of the stories in the Word. After the earthquake, when I read Matthew, I was hoping for wisdom and hoping for a restored relationship with the Lord. The stories I read—little stars of truth—began to assemble themselves in my mind and touch my heart. They brought me through the night, back to day.

For Signs, Seasons, and Days

My experience during this time helps illustrate the idea that the seasons of the heart—the waxing and waning of faith, or the dawning and setting of feeling God's presence in our lives—are for our own benefit. I was not ready to accept what had happened or even be consoled; and as someone who understands God to be the author and director of all, on an unconscious level, I blamed him. I was not ready to be close to God, so he allowed me the space that my grief was demanding. Sometimes, distance from God is God's mercy.

The Lord allows us to enter into those very dark times in our lives, because having only positive experiences can lead to indifference and undervaluation of what is good. I never thought anything at all about clean, running water and uninterrupted access to electricity until I moved to Nepal, where electricity is intermittent and the water—when there is water—is not potable. We can sometimes take what is good for granted. Unvaried exposure to favorable conditions can also lead to a sense of entitlement; we become spoiled. We are allowed to experience spiritually dark times so that we don't become ungrateful. Our relationship with the Lord must move through organic cycles of closeness and distance for us to grow spiritually.

These variations also protect us. The closer we get to the Lord, the more we realize our complete dependence on him for our existence. We become faced with the fact that all progress and all that is good in our lives are only ever of the Lord and not at all of ourselves. These truths pose a tremendous threat to the ego. Like a threatened, cornered animal, the ego would come to despise and fear the Lord without the gift of time apart, the nighttimes of our spirit. We absolutely must retain our sense of self and autonomy. Just as we need physical sleep, we also need spiritual night and sleep. The Lord's absence, then, is in fact the Lord's presence—yet another expression of his perfect love for us.

During other dark nights, I have been fully conscious of my anger at God for restricting my freedom. Seeing others live seemingly freer lives filled with contentment and ease, I felt fenced in. The Lord threatens the ego, so the closer we feel to the Lord, the more rebellious our sense of self becomes. And this sometimes feels like taking one step forward and one step back: the closer we get to the Lord, the more demons we experience. However, we can reimagine this dance as the evolving seasons of the soul. Every time we draw closer, we see the darkness of our selfishness. Proximity to divine love shines a bright light on those darker elements of selfhood that otherwise would have remained hidden from sight. Our selfishness does not want to be let go, so it becomes rebellious. With the passage of time and exposure to more divine sunlight, though, the presence of that particular form of selfishness, or demon, wanes until it no longer has any power in our lives. As Jesus entered deeper into his divinity, the Devil came to tempt him; and Jesus overcame.

The Lord permits us to fall asleep to his presence so that we don't have to constantly come to terms with the sensation of our nothingness in the presence of the I AM. The sun sets, and we fall asleep spiritually. These times of distance from the Lord are like a moonlit night. Sometimes, the Lord even allows for moonless nights during those times when we need even more distance from him.

When the moon of the spiritual realm enters its darkest phase, the Lord continues to guide us through the nighttime of our soul. Once the Lord has evolved us to **Day 4,** the commandments telling us not to steal, lie, murder, commit adultery, or covet are all the more present and established in our thinking. These are guiding stars. We won't forget that we should live with compassion for others. In fact, the culmination of the processes of **Days 1, 2, 3,** and **4** establishes within us a true love for others and for what is good. These gifts from the Lord guide us and protect us within his love, even when we don't feel faith or love for the Lord. For millennia, people have used stars to navigate at night. So, too, the stars that shine into our spirit guide us through the night, until dawn. Even in our darkest nights, the sun still blazes upon us; like the rotating earth, it is we who have turned our spiritual face away from God.

There are many verses in the Bible that talk about the darkening of the sun and moon and about the stars being cast down to the earth. In Matthew 24:29, for example, Jesus says, "Immediately after the suffering of those days the sun will be darkened, and the moon will not give its light; the stars will fall from heaven, and the powers of heaven will be shaken." Passages such as this one describe a difficult and terrible spiritual state that we must pass through. The darkening of the sun indicates a state in which we can no longer sense the Lord as real. The moon failing to give light symbolizes a state in which we no longer have faith in the Lord or even have a recollection of the Lord's goodness. The stars falling from heaven represent knowledge about God being degraded so that it no longer guides us back to the Lord; rather, our knowledge seems to consist of mere empty facts.

In the book of Revelation, the sun, moon, and stars are depicted as integral elements of a living, radiant "woman clothed with the sun" (12:1). The moon under her feet represents how when we stand on faith, we experience a radiant, vibrant, and selfless spiritual love for both the Lord and for others. That she is clothed with the sun represents that eventually, the Lord's love is present within us as our very life and shines out of us with warmth toward others. The crown of stars represents wisdom, knowledge, and understanding of the Word and of life. The woman herself represents the Lord's bride, his church that is living both within his people and within individuals in whom true spiritual love has been established. Though we are not each of us the Lord's bride, she can live within each and every one of us.

In the same story from the book of Revelation, it is the "great red dragon, with seven heads and ten horns" (12:3) that casts the stars to the ground. This dragon represents our faith in the senses, which amplifies and glorifies our sense of self. It is this faith in our sensory experience of the natural world that destroys our spiritual life, as described by the darkening and casting down of the heavenly bodies.

Inviting in the Daylight

Day 4 can be seen as the tipping point in our spiritual evolution. **Days 1, 2,** and **3** involve escaping the misery and confusion of an ego-based life and resolving spiritual problems that often tie in with psychological problems. These three days are characterized by the hard work of our own efforts. **Day 4** is not about solving problems or about working hard; it describes a spiritual awakening from the delusion of self into the joy of knowing the Lord's love.

Jesus is eager to unite with us: "Listen! I am standing at the door, knocking; if you hear my voice and open the door, I will come in to you and eat with you, and you with me" (Revelation 3:20). He also explains what we need to do to really encounter him: "They who have my commandments and keep them are those who love me; and those who love me will be loved by my Father, and I will love them and reveal myself to them" (John 14:21). To get to **Day 4,** we have to go through the hard work of **Days 1, 2,** and **3.**

SUGGESTED PRACTICES

This chapter is primarily about experiencing the Lord in a direct and meaningful way, one in which his divine truth shines into our minds and his love warms our lives. **Day 4** shows us the faith that illumines our steps at those times when we feel furthest away from the Lord, as well as the spiritual knowledge by which we can navigate our way back to him even during the darkest times—like sailors at sea or the wise men of the East. The task for this chapter is to deepen our relationship with the Lord.

Cultivating Awareness in Daily Activities

1

Continue practicing Lord-centered mindfulness (see pages 110–11, above) as a way of developing a sensation of the Lord's immediate, loving presence.

2

Spend some time watching a sunrise, a sunset, or the night sky, with gratitude toward the Lord and recalling the spiritual counterparts of these natural phenomena. Consider how the Lord has used your weaknesses and burdens as a way of moving you from **Day 3** to **Day 4** in some area of your life.

3

Working to see the Lord within other people is a wonderful and powerful form of Lord-centered mindfulness. The Lord is in the least of us all (and we are all equally least), so whenever in conversation with someone, recognize that individual as a vessel for the Lord. What is the Lord teaching in this encounter? How can you best serve the Lord in this situation?

Meditative Practice

Day 4 is about encountering the Lord and praying for him to become emotionally and intellectually real in our life. This meditation will entail a visualization of encountering the Lord. Visualizing this meeting is a form of prayer that employs the imagination rather than words. For the Lord to shine into our lives as a sun, warming our hearts and illuminating our minds, we must be able to move beyond words into images and forms. Words are primarily tools of the intellect; a fuller, more personal experience of God, though, must also be a matter of the heart. Therefore, this meditation is designed to help you experience the Lord not just in the intellectual, verbal part of your mind but also in your heart.

Let's begin with the induction.

[Perform Meditation Induction 2 (p. 59, above)]

Meditation—**Day 4:** Encountering God

From within this meditative state, listen to the following prayer and let it fill your mind: "Hail the sun of righteousness, risen with healing in his wings! Lord, we pray for your healing love to dawn in fullness into our lives. We invite you into our heart. Please come in."

[Pause for 30 seconds; then read the following]

From Revelation 3:
Listen! I am standing at the door, knocking; if you hear my voice and open the door, I will come in to you and eat with you, and you with me.

[Pause for a moment]

ooooo

The Lord is always here, now, immediately present with you. He is by the door of your heart, waiting for you to open up, as best you can, so that he can commune with you.

[Pause for 30 seconds]

In the following description, let your imagination lead the way.

See yourself in a room made of wood and with large windows. Sunlight is streaming in through the windows, bathing a table that has a chair on either side of it. Take a seat in one of the chairs and then take a moment to simply be, soaking in the sunlight.

[Pause for 30 seconds]

Now, let these words fill your mind: "Lord, please enter my heart. Please become real to me. Please awaken me to your light and fill my life with your love. Let me know you. Enlighten me and enliven me." With each breath, repeat these words to yourself: "Lord, please enter my life. Please awaken me to know you."

[Pause for 1 minute]

In the quiet that follows, imagine that you hear a knock at the door. Go to the door and open it. Bow as you open the door to the Lord. Invite the Lord to enter, and allow the encounter to continue to unfold without trying to direct it.

Doing Practice

1

During the **Day 4** period, make your best effort at loving others in the same way that the Lord loves you—being non-judgmental, all-forgiving, encouraging, and warm. When we can be loving toward others, the Lord is awakening us to his all-embracing love—**Day 3** must precede **Day 4**. Since your relationships with those closest to you tend to be the ones that are impacted most deeply by what you do and what you say, it may be best to start practicing the Lord's love with family and friends.

If we do not forgive, we cannot experience the Lord. This is explained quite succinctly in the Bible when the Lord says, "Do not judge, so that you may not be judged. For with the judgment you make you will be judged, and the measure you give will be the measure you get" (Matthew 7:1–2). It is not that the Lord holds a grudge against us; instead, it is our grudge against others that blocks our ability to feel the Lord's selfless love. Therefore, to feel the Lord's immediate presence, we must forgive.

Developing upon the forgiveness task in **Day 3** and in the spirit of the Lord's all-forgiving nature, try to extend your compassion to more than just one person. Make a list of five people against whom you hold a grudge. Take some time actively working to forgive them, or at least one or two of them. Note that this process may not always involve forgiving them face to face. You may consider writing them a letter, just as you did as part of the task in **Day 3.** Some helpful tools include praying for the Lord to give you a forgiving spirit; remembering our own transgressions, especially, when applicable, those similar to the ones we fault the others for; contemplating the idea that all people are born into delusion and that before it can be dispersed, selfish and harmful behavior will inevitably occur; and considering the fact that people do the best they can with the heredity and experiences that make up their lives. The Lord's path for each individual is different, so we must be tolerant of the paths that others tread. Using these tools, we can feel empathy for the conditions of others and in turn have greater success at coming to peace with those who need our forgiveness. A final tool is praying for the other party's well-being. We can't pray for someone and hold a grudge against them at the same time.

2

The Lord states that "when you are offering your gift at the altar, if you remember that your brother or sister has something against you, leave your gift there before the altar and go; first be reconciled to your brother or sister, and then come and offer your gift" (Matthew 5:23–24). To experience the Lord's love, we need to make our best effort to be right with others whom we have harmed. If we do not make amends, either guilt or self-righteousness will inhibit our ability to feel the Lord's loving presence in our lives. While guilt causes us to hide from the Lord, self-righteousness is a rejection of God. Sometimes we may not even recognize that we have guilt or are self-righteous about something we've done. It can be valuable to take a bit of time to search the heart.

Just as you did for those who harmed you, make a list of those you have harmed but to whom you have not yet made amends. Then, do what you can to make reparations to at least one of these people. You may wish to include more of the people on the list. Sometimes a simple apology will suffice, but sometimes more will be required, such as acts of kindness, monetary compensation, or the performance of services. If you are unable for whatever reason to communicate directly with those you have wronged, in the spirit of reparation, try doing good deeds for those who you know have been wronged by others in perhaps a similar way.

3

A final and very vital practice I recommend is reading the Word of God and meditating on its meaning in your life. You might consider complementing this chapter's suggested practices, in particular, with the Gospel of Matthew.

ooooo

This chapter includes many suggested practices. If doing them all seems overwhelming, do just the ones that seem possible for you in the time that you have available. You can always return to the others at a later date.

Suggested Questions for Pondering
and/or Discussion

- In your efforts at Lord-centered mindfulness, were you able to feel the Lord's presence in a deeper way than you otherwise have been able to do in the past? Did you discover anything that is keeping you from experiencing the Lord in a firsthand, loving way?

- How would you compare your experience of asking for forgiveness with that of forgiving others? Did either one make you feel closer to the Lord? Was one or the other noticeably more difficult to do? Did one influence the other in any way?

- Is there anything about the Word of God that keeps you feeling distant from the Lord? Does your view on the suffering of life keep you from trusting the Lord? Do you carry any mental or emotional burdens that keep you from either feeling or wanting to be closer to the Lord?

- Has the Lord used your weaknesses and burdens to draw you closer to a relationship with him? If so, in what ways was this experience more or less difficult than you expected it to be?

- Have you ever had an experience of the Lord's selfless love? If so, what did it feel like?

- Have you ever met someone who seems to have a clear sense of the Lord's love? How might that inform the way he or she relates to others? What can you learn from that individual? In what ways might you change your thoughts, attitude, and lifestyle in order to reach that clearer sense?

- Think about a quality that you admire about yourself. Does the idea of losing that quality frighten you? Why or why not?

- How did you find the exercise of trying to love others as the Lord loves you? Did you notice any differences in making these efforts toward friends and family versus toward strangers?

- Do you have any further reflections concerning this chapter?

DAY 5: LEARNING TO SWIM AND LEARNING TO FLY

And God said, "Let the waters bring forth swarms of living creatures, and let birds fly above the earth across the dome of the sky." So God created the great sea monsters and every living creature that moves, of every kind, with which the waters swarm, and every winged bird of every kind. And God saw that it was good. God blessed them, saying, "Be fruitful and multiply and fill the waters in the seas, and let birds multiply on the earth." And there was evening and there was morning, the fifth day.

(Genesis 1:20–23)

My wife and I both love birds, and Nepal is an excellent place for bird-watching. There is a greater variety of bird species there than in any other nation—impressive for a country about the size of Iowa. Many avian aficionados come from around the world to visit Nepal. Though only a small portion of that vast variety graced our neighborhood, we kept our gaze trained upward in hopes of sighting one of our many aerial friends. We loved to catch a rare glimpse of the brilliant crimson and yellow of the minivets and to watch the funny antics of the green parrots. The beautiful song of the oriental magpie-robin and the tell-tale *rat-a-tat-tat* that led us to the ladder-backed woodpecker brought smiles to our faces. To see the porcelain-white egrets slide silently through sapphire skies speaks peace to the listening heart.

Flashing their brilliant colors and singing out songs of joy, birds are not bound to the ponderous stuff of earth; they fill the skies with grace, beauty, and unfettered freedom. It is not hard to discern the spiritual symbolism expressed by birds: that rising up above the ego gives us a higher degree of vision, which opens us up to greater joy and freedom.

As we will discuss in more detail later, while **Days 2** and **3** parallel **Days 5** and **6** of our spiritual evolution, between these stages, there is a distinct change that occurs to our relationship with our sense of selfhood. In **Day 3,** with our thoughts reaching up to God and our hands reaching out to serve others, it may have seemed that our journey was nearly done. Our thoughts and behaviors were improving, but real spiritual vitality was still lacking. Just as trees are rooted in the earth, so all of our spiritual efforts and behaviors were still rooted in a belief that the self is capable of achieving something spiritual. Just as flora represents our rootedness in creating a foundation for our spiritual growth, fauna represents the vitality in our genuine spiritual efforts, a vitality that comes from above. Imagine a great piano student who spends seven hours a day practicing. She can sight-read with great accuracy, but her teacher tells her that she still hasn't arrived—that she lacks fluidity, passion, and freedom. After another year of practicing regularly, the student comes to understand what her teacher meant. Before, when she played, she drove each note into existence with her conscious mind; now rather than the sensation of playing the music, she feels the music alive and playing *through* her. She is liberated from having to focus on controlling what her fingers do. Rather than it being an intellectual effort toward correctness, her performance is now mostly a fluid experience of the heart, with the intellect quietly working on a more subconscious level.

That's how I envision what happens during **Days 2** and **3** to be different from where we are in **Days 5** and **6**. But what effects the change between these two stages in our evolution? **Day 4,** of course. In **Day 4,** feeling the immediate, loving presence of a human God ushers in a sense of oneness both with the Lord and with our fellow human beings. Firsthand experience of the loving God supersedes in its power and vitality all other experiences, and so faith in selfhood is never again the same. It is on this day that we truly see and feel that it is the Lord, and not we ourselves, who is able to love, to have faith, to *do* anything at all, or even to exist. When love is playing out in our lives, we come to know that it exists of its own accord and that we are merely means for its expression. God is the I AM, the beginning and the end—a perspective that is radically different than the egocentric one we had when we began this journey. The difference between egocentrism and God's perspective is the difference between spiritual death and spiritual life.

Before **Day 4,** we saw the universe as a dead machine; from **Day 4** on, we are awake and see it as a vibrant, evolving expression of the Lord's love. Once confusing and threatening, life now shows itself to be a beautiful flow toward our destiny of peace and love. The self no longer peers fearfully and critically out at others; instead, we look at others and at our relationships as sacred. Focusing on right and wrong is replaced with focusing on how to serve and bless; within this love, avoiding what is harmful is a given goal. Self-based comparisons of who is better and who is best no longer make sense. Before, we wondered how far along we were in our spiritual journey or how close to heaven we had reached, but these questions no longer make sense; it's not about the destination, because we see that the journey itself *is* the revelation of heaven—that heaven is in the here and now. Nothing looks the same, and it all looks a lot better.

It's a Matter of Perspective

Our new bird's-eye view even rearranges our perspective on the past. Knowing that all is held within the gentle progressive flow of the Lord's river of life, the traumas and terrors of our past are now recognized as tiles within the much larger and astoundingly mysterious mosaic of life. Ultimately, each failure and injury is used by the Lord for good; and with our new point of view, world history is altered in such a way that divine providence becomes more clear. The evolving presence of God's love is seen not only in the amazing progression of the evolution of the physical universe and of life on earth but also in the steady overall improvement of human society. It flows silently and secretly through and within all of reality; it sustains reality, as it *is* reality. This is not to say that we can let go and let the flow take care of everything. The central instrument through which divine love evolves society is the sense of self. The critical state of the environment will not solve itself without our proactive involvement. The pianist must still sit down at the piano and play even after she becomes aware that she is a vessel for the music, not its creator. I enjoy writing music, and I often feel that the music itself tells me what to write, though it is still my mind and body that must bring it out to be heard.

This new, higher perspective sings out a new future as well. We know that the Lord is leading all toward good, even if we cannot immediately see that goodness. Jesus speaks to this idea in a number of ways. Having had personal experience with a living human God allows us to better understand such statements of his as:

> Consider the ravens: they neither sow nor reap, they have neither storehouse nor barn, and yet God feeds them. Of how much more value are you than the birds! (Luke 12:24)

> When a woman is in labor, she has pain, because her hour has come. But when her child is born, she no longer

remembers the anguish because of the joy of having brought a human being into the world. So you have pain now; but I will see you again, and your hearts will rejoice, and no one will take your joy from you. (John 16:21–22)

When lifted above an egocentric state of mind, we feel the truth of these comforting quotes—we are held by God's loving providence. Not just these quotes, but all of Scripture may take on new meaning for us.

It is not difficult to see how this new perspective on all areas of life is represented by birds, as a quick overview of their taxonomic hierarchy will demonstrate. For example, the new overarching perspective that life is guided toward good by the Lord might be considered a *family*. A *genus* within that perspective might be the understanding that even upsetting events are used by the Lord to bring us toward eternal happiness. And a *species* of that *genus* might be any one of the countless nuanced situations in which certain thoughts take wing within our mind, filling the skies of our higher consciousness with an increasingly diverse array of meanings that are specific to those situations in our life. And the individual bird, of course, is any one of those higher thoughts (e.g., *As I look for a job, I can trust in God.*).

The Difference between Birds and Fish

While this new elevated perspective is a true perspective, it does not eclipse—at least not permanently—our persistent tendency toward egoic desires and thoughts. As darkness is part of our design, we will inevitably slip back into the judgment and fear of our self-oriented delusion; but when we do, we can now better see that our faults and failings are not the end of the world but instead are fertilizer for new life.

Though we are never going to be without a lower, ego-based mind, we are no longer wholly driven by its delusion. Fish represent our newfound freedom to navigate the waters below, the lower thoughts and emotions of ego-based consciousness. In other words, birds in flight represent those intellectual ideas about spirit that bring us freedom and happiness, and fish represent our ability to swim gracefully through the currents of self-based consciousness. There is a difference between experiencing the joy of intellectual vision and applying that vision to the currents of emotion and desire that flow through the lower mind. Fish represent a change in how we approach our own mind, how we navigate the emotional realm within. Recently, I had a financial setback. I had to pray for trust and recall the Lord's statements that I need not worry about what I will wear or eat and that I can't serve both God and money. It helped me enter a more peaceful state. I also experienced frustration over the fact that I couldn't do what I wanted to do, which was spend time outside, because I had to take care of the financial situation. Again, I had to remind myself to trust in providence and to surrender my will to what God requires of my time. It helped.

Just as fish need water to live, we actually need self-based thinking—the waters below—to grow and thrive. God doesn't want us sitting on clouds and strumming harps of gold; he wants us to use the gifts he has given us in order to face those obstacles that will challenge us and in turn evolve us. Love is proven in the living. Wisdom is known by her children.

How we navigate our own mind is much more intimately bound to the circumstances of our daily life than are the intellectual ideas themselves that we use to do the navigating. For example, when a loved one passes away, when our marriage is severely strained, or when we see our child suffering in some way, it affects us on a personal level. During times like these, the intellectual idea that all things lead to good probably seems remote at best. We might even consider this idea to be insensitive to the acute pain we are feeling—just as the words "you'll feel better soon" don't mean much to a person who is experiencing the physical agony of having shattered a bone.

As I talked about in **Day 4,** in the wake of the Nepal earthquake, on an intellectual level, not much had changed for me. I still held the same vision of God and his relationship to life, within which suffering and tragedy had a meaningful place. Intellectually, I did not doubt God or his goodness. I did, however, notice that I had lost interest in making contact with God or with anything spiritual. Instead, I had become focused on what needed to get done to help those around me. More than a month later, feelings of anguish and anger arose. Despite a strong faith in the goodness of God and an intellectually satisfying answer to how such suffering is acceptable, the emotions under the surface of my consciousness were operating within a system as different from the intellect as are the currents of the ocean from the winds of the sky.

I began to wonder what was going on in my spirit. My actions were not about God; in fact, they were not spiritually motivated at all. Instead, I felt focused on the natural world and the people I was with, to the exclusion of any thought or even care about God. I didn't pray, read, meditate, or do anything spiritual for at least a month. I even felt liberated, in a way—free from having to make the effort required to lead an intentional, spiritual life.

What I did feel was love and appreciation for the people I was meeting. I felt a great joy interacting with them and being able to offer something of value. Those living feelings of deep connection do not arise from the emotions of the self; they cannot arise from the self any more than fish are created from the water in which they swim. So though I did not feel God's presence, he was still present in a way that I could not recognize. He animated me with feelings of love so that he could help people who needed help. My hostility toward God had later changed into indifference, which was the current—the water itself—of the lower, self-oriented mind. The lower mind will do what it will do. I had no sense of making any effort to temper my emotions with reason. I simply felt inspired to help others as best I could. And that's the beauty of the life of spirit—it slips in without us noticing and lives through us despite ourselves, or more accurately, regardless of ourselves. The self is the vehicle for the life of spirit, just as water is the vehicle for fish.

Strangely enough, the sense of indifference and anger that I felt toward God may have actually been part of God's way of motivating me to get up and help. If I had felt content with God, then I probably would not have done as much work—*God is good . . . he'll take care of it.* Obviously, all of this was going on far below my consciousness, which again illustrates the point that our spiritual life is being evolved by God alone, regardless of the self. The fish keep swimming, even as the ocean rages.

With these symbols of birds and fish, I can have a better understanding of that experience. From a spiritual perspective, the birds of the sky, the intellectual concepts that reveal God to be good, don't have an obvious, direct relationship to the life under the waters. When our consciousness is operating from within this intellectual space, we see our own emotions—the waters—in an intellectually removed way; but we don't see the life within them. We are looking at the waters but don't see the fish. We can see and love spiritual truth without knowing how it might be moving within us. Perhaps the best way to explain the relationship between birds and fish is to say that birds are the ability to give God-oriented intellectual meaning to reality, and fish are the ability to move through the lower mind of day-to-day activity according to a God-based orientation. They both have to do with making life meaningful, but they function in totally different ways and play out in totally different areas of living.

So why does the Lord cloak his motivation for goodness within our unconscious? Why are the fish hidden in the depths instead of being visible at the surface? I think the answer is that were we to regularly see these living motives driving our actions in the same way we can see intellectual concepts, we'd too easily identify with them as our own. We'd take credit for them, take them for granted, and in turn destroy them. It is like what is happening today in the oceans of the world: since we can find the fish, we hunt them to extinction. Their survival depends on their invisibility. Jesus says of good motives and good deeds, "Do not let your left hand know what your right hand is doing" (Matthew 6:3). In other words, it is a good thing that the intellect is blind to what is motivating us—at least at the time when it is doing so. Knowledge is power and power is not always good. God needs to be the one who orchestrates and evolves love within our lives. As soon as the self gets involved, it cannot be love.

Paradoxically, the further we move away from having faith in the ego, the greater the *sense* of power and autonomy we experience. To the extent that we realize we are in and of ourselves completely lifeless, we gain an increasing *sense* of vitality. We no longer trust our negative emotions, attitudes, desires, and thoughts to be valid; and in turn, we experience the happiness, freedom, and sense of vitality that are all derived from selfless love. In **Day 5,** we know we are inherently void of self-life and yet the state of our spirit is described by means of beautiful, moving, living creatures. God wants to fill us to the point at which we are overflowing with the sensation of life, joy, and freedom. For this to happen without dire consequence, we must first be separated from the delusion of selfhood. We must die in order to live.

The Lord alone is self-existing and so the Lord alone is life: "We are not life in itself; we are just organs that receive life.

The Lord is life in itself" (*True Christianity* §461:3). Therefore, all that lives is animated by the Lord's life, which is selfless love. Thus, our increasing sense of vitality comes from an increase in the presence and influence of the Lord's selfless love within our lives. We are beginning to see things from the perspective of selfless love—a perspective that, though borrowed, fills us with *actual* life. This view consists of spiritually animated insights, an overarching vision of reality, and the ability to think one's way through and against the flow of negative and harmful emotions.

"Be fruitful and multiply . . ."

Just as our **Day 3** efforts grow and multiply, so also in **Day 5** do our intellectual insights and ability to navigate the lower mind perpetuate themselves and increase. Jesus makes this process clear to us when he says that "the kingdom of heaven is like a mustard seed that someone took and sowed in his field; it is the smallest of all the seeds, but when it has grown it is the greatest of shrubs and becomes a tree, so that the birds of the air come and make nests in its branches" (Matthew 13:31–32). The kingdom of God, according to Jesus, "is like yeast that a woman took and mixed in with three measures of flour until all of it was leavened" (Luke 13:21). The Lord's love inside of us multiplies itself, and our ability to think clearly from a spiritual perspective likewise increases: "the birds of the air come and make nests in its branches."

SUGGESTED PRACTICES

This chapter describes how God evolves us so that our thoughts see God's presence and guidance in our lives and in all of life. God evolves our lower mind in such a way that we are able to, with intention, move toward good things, even against the currents of selfishness.

Cultivating Awareness in Daily Activities

1

As Jesus said in Matthew 6:26, "Look at the birds of the air." Spend some time mindfully watching birds. Try to connect with the spiritual message they offer you. You may wish to go to a park, forest, or other special place where a great number of birds might be found. Or you may want to simply watch the birds in your own backyard.

2

Spend a day observing your typical perspective on and general attitude toward reality. What types of messages make up your internal banter? Are your thoughts positive and reassuring, or do they repeat messages of doubt and despair? In either case, having a Lord-centered message to recite to yourself can keep you aloft. Write down the following words or, better yet, some personally meaningful quote from the Word, and then try spending the next day reciting the message to yourself, either silently or aloud, as often as possible: "The Lord is all-loving, omniscient, and omnipotent. All of reality is within his stream of providence. The Lord is life, so life is perfect. I choose, therefore, to see reality as perfect."

Repeating such fundamental, life-affirming truths to ourselves helps make them real for us. We begin to see life through them and so can live according to them.

3

Practice gratitude. Gratitude lifts us up above our ego-centered concerns. Throughout your day, be determined to thank the Lord for each experience and event that you encounter. Keep present in your mind those things for which you are grateful.

Meditative Practice

In this meditation, you will be invited to rise up above the ego-oriented consciousness in order to experience the freedom and joy of a higher perspective, one that is alive with trust in the Lord and the life of the Lord. Bringing this perspective to your day-to-day activities will help you to navigate the waters of your lower mind.

Let's begin with the induction.

[Perform Meditation Induction 2 (p. 59, above)]

Meditation—**Day 5:** Learning to Swim and Learning to Fly

From within this meditative state, allow your mind to open up to a particular problem or worry that you currently face.

[Pause for 20 seconds]

Now, for each of the following questions, allow an answer to emerge in your mind.

What is the outcome you fear?

[Pause for 15 to 20 seconds]

Who will experience its repercussions?

[Pause for 15 to 20 seconds]

In what ways will they be affected? What particular hardships might they end up facing?

[Pause for 30 seconds]

Now, I invite you to recognize that these hardships, by God's will and providence, will perhaps not come to pass.

[Pause for 20 seconds]

I invite you to trust that even if these difficulties are in fact unavoidable, they will eventually, somehow be used for the eternal well-being of those involved. Sometimes this requires a leap of faith. I invite you to make that leap of faith in this moment.

[Pause for 1 minute]

In going through times of trouble, a person may become more empathetic or grow stronger in their ability to cope; they may gain a higher perspective on the world around them, or they may become closer to God in recognizing his all-embracing love.

[Pause for 10 seconds]

How might these particular difficulties, then, be brought to eventual good by the Lord? And how might they serve the eternal welfare of those involved?

[Pause for 30 seconds]

Now, take three or four slow and deep breaths. Imagine each exhalation as a way of expelling fear and each inhalation as a way of drawing the Lord near, drawing trust into your life. Surrender yourself to the moment and receive peace.

[Pause for 1 minute]

Now, imagine that you are holding the problem in your hands and that you see it transform into a dove. Gently release the bird from your hands, and watch it fly upward to the light of the Lord.

[Pause for 30 seconds]

Seeing from a higher perspective will not take away all of the problems and pain, but it can put these experiences into the Lord's hands, where we know that all will be bent and used for good. Whenever you start to become worried or upset, place these feelings into the bigger picture of the Lord's love, and let him help you navigate the currents of the lower mind so that you may rise up above the waters on the wings of eagles.

[Pause for 10 seconds]

Now, repeat the following mantra with each breath, entering the meaning of the words as fully and genuinely as you can: Breathing in, say to yourself, "Please enter, Lord . . ." Breathing out, say, "I trust you, Lord, and fear not . . ."

[Pause for 15 seconds]

In the quiet that follows, breathe in and out slowly and deeply.

Doing Practice

According to Swedenborg, fish represent truths of faith. When these truths of faith come to life in our mind, they begin to have dominion over the tossing and turning waters of our lower thoughts. For example, the feeling of worthlessness can be tempered and even overcome by saying to oneself, "God created and loves me. I have purpose and value, even when I can't feel this to be so." Thinking that someone doesn't deserve to be forgiven or delighting in seeing hardship strike a person can also be corrected with truths of faith: "God has forgiven me so much; I, too, must forgive." Inhibitory fear can be countered with the truth that the Lord is in charge and is good. During the **Day 5** period, try to remain attentive to the fish that swim deep beneath the current, and see if you can temper your typically automatic reactions to day-to-day experiences.

Suggested Questions for Pondering
and/or Discussion

- What was it like to "look at the birds of the air" and meditate on their spiritual meaning? Why did Jesus urge us to observe birds in flight? What do you discern in God's Word as it is written in nature around us?

- Were you able to hold on to any specific ideas based in faith and use them to successfully navigate the waters of the lower mind? If so, what were those truths and how did they help?

- Did reciting a life-affirming quote have an impact on your day? Did it have an impact on your understanding of the words themselves?

- How did being mindful of practicing gratitude affect your days?

- Do you have any further reflections concerning this chapter?

DAY 6: ANIMATED BY LOVE

And God said, "Let the earth bring forth living creatures of every kind:
cattle and creeping things and wild animals of the earth of every kind."
And it was so. God made the wild animals of the earth of every kind, and
the cattle of every kind, and everything that creeps upon the ground of
every kind. And God saw that it was good.

(Genesis 1:24–25)

Since physical reality is the ultimate manifestation of spiritual reality, as we will discuss at the end of this book, it seems no coincidence that the evolution of the earth demonstrates a similar pattern to the progression described in the Creation story. It is believed that before plant life consumed carbon dioxide and produced oxygen in significant amounts, the earth's atmosphere was murky, with only diffuse light filtering down to the planet's surface, and the sun, moon, and stars would not have been visible. After plants and the appearance of the sun came fish, birds, and then, finally, animals.

The pattern we see in the relationship between **Days 1, 2,** and **3** is the same as what we see in the relationship between **Days 4, 5,** and **6:** illumination (**Days 1** and **4**); developments in the waters below and in the skies above (**Days 2** and **5**); and then developments on the land (**Days 3** and **6**). Likewise, there is a relationship between **Days 0** and **7,** as Creation is book-ended by a lack of activity: the pre-illuminative state of **Day 0** represents stasis, the moment before the first rays of spiritual light, and **Day 7,** the Sabbath, represents our ultimate place of rest. From a spiritual perspective, these patterns describe insight that leads to new ways of thinking, which in turn leads to a change in heart and to new ways of living. The difference between **Days 1, 2,** and **3** and **Days 4, 5,** and **6** is the essential motivation and spirit behind what occurs. In the first series, our spiritual evolution is heavily cloaked by the delusion of selfhood—we think that it is we ourselves who see the light; we think that it is we ourselves who do work in discerning between higher and lower forms of thinking; and we think that it is we ourselves who are responsible for our good efforts.

The insight of **Day 4,** that the Lord alone is the doer, leads to the new ways of thinking that are represented by birds and fish in **Day 5.** In this state—in which we have a personal, deep encounter with the Lord—we are able to think about life from an elevated perspective (birds) and even from within the arena of the ever-present self-based mind (fish), and this leads to a change in heart. We are for the first time *animated* with the spirit of the Lord's genuine, selfless love. We serve people not because it is the right thing to do, but because we feel love for others. We live morally not because it is the law, but because we don't want to harm anyone. We work hard because we genuinely want to serve society. Love is now flowing through our heart and mind into our actions. We are free.

These new *animations* of the heart and mind are the living *animals* that are created in **Day 6.** They are not *rooted in* the ground like trees, but instead they *move upon* the earth. We are given to experience genuine selfless love as if it was our own, yet at the same time we know it to actually be the Lord's life within us, animating us. This vital, selfless love welling up in our heart is as different from the old motivations and efforts to live rightly as is animal life from vegetable life. With the animations of **Day 5**, birds and fish symbolize things of the mind—higher, expansive insights and vision, which are alive with spirit, and the ability to navigate the swells of emotions with spiritual agility. The animations of **Day 6**, on the other hand, are those of the heart—affection for the well-being of others and society at large, as well as countless varieties of the general desire to bless others, society, country, and ultimately the Lord's kingdom of love on earth.

People sometimes use the phrase *"warm fuzzies"* when they are describing feelings of love. Animals are both warm and fuzzy. Physical warmth is a universal symbol for love, which is spiritual warmth, and this can be seen in much of the language that we use to describe such feelings. We might say that we are *warming up* to something when we mean that we are growing to like it. We also very often use the word *warm* to describe people who are loving. If the warmth of animals represents the primary quality of love, then their fuzziness is the comfort that love brings—both to the giver and to the receiver. It feels good to have the Lord's selfless goodwill animating our actions; it feels warm and fuzzy. Animals not only represent love, but they evoke love; almost everyone loves and is moved by animals. The qualities they represent seem to stir these same spiritual qualities within us.

The Lord's Love *Is* Our Freedom

Having the Lord's love live within our heart also gives us new spiritual freedom. When our actions are rooted in the ego, we are always expecting something in return, wondering what we'll receive as a reward. When what we do comes out of a genuine desire to bless others, though, we are truly free. We are free because such actions are spontaneous rather than calculated in terms of self-based motives. When we expect something in return for our good deeds, such as praise or reciprocity, we miss out on the joy that is inherent in loving and serving others. The sense of self turns prosocial activity into a business transaction with an internal, often unnoticed, book of accounts. As a result, if things aren't adding up in our favor, we become frustrated and feel trapped; we often end up doing things in accordance with the hidden selfish agenda. When these types of motivations are put aside, however, our actions become based in a genuine love for others, and we experience the joy of this love and the actions that come out of it. Experiencing this joy *is* true freedom, because there are no strings attached. Unlike selfish desires, which are often hidden because they are socially unacceptable, genuine love for others can be given free reign over our lives without ill consequence—just as animals move freely over the surface of the earth, going where they want when they want. And rather than having to struggle against our ego-based nature to live a life of goodness, we can simply do what we want because we want what is good; we encounter no limits. Genuine love is freedom itself because it depends on nothing outside itself; it only wants to give of itself without any concern about what it might receive in return. Regardless of everything else that happens in our lives, we can always try to bless others. The only barrier that prevents us from doing so is our own ego.

Living Creatures

There are hundreds of species of animals, yet all of them are interconnected to make a valuable whole representing the great diversity of ways in which love can manifest. Three kinds of animals are described in Genesis 1:24–25: *cattle, creeping things,* and *wild animals.* It may at times seem excessive to search for the inner meaning in every detail of the Bible; but since the Word of God is a divine parable describing our spiritual evolution, then we have to wonder why these three types of animals are specified.

The first of the living creatures to be brought forth are cattle, generally gentle and tamable animals that serve us directly and profoundly in many ways. Cows provide us with such foods as dairy products and beef, and their skins provide us with leather. I understand cattle to represent those kinds of love that are most obviously and directly beneficial to human society—for example, a strong love in marriage; a special love for family and for nurturing children; or a passion for defending the downtrodden. All of these types of love focus on helping people through direct action and through forming intimate relationships. Just as cattle and other domesticated animals have a very close relationship with human beings, these types of love are near to God's love. According to Swedenborg, cattle, in this context, "symbolize the good, gentle things in us . . . feelings of affection" (*Secrets of Heaven* §45).

After the cattle come the creeping things. It should be noted that the term translated as *creeping thing* can equally be translated as *moving thing,* and so we can understand the term as referring to animals that move more freely about the earth. Selfless love can also take on forms that are more removed from the close relationships that we form in service to others. The more practical and intellectual pursuits—or, as Swedenborg says, "what the intellect grasps" (§44)—that inspire us in our professional lives not only stimulate us but are also very useful, helping society to function at a higher level. These loves of the world, which are more engaged with our everyday affairs, are represented by those creatures that move around in all directions.

The third and final of the living creatures are wild animals. While cattle represent an immediate love for others, and creeping things represent a love for the pursuits of the world that bless our lives, wild animals represent that kind of love that can be dangerous and difficult to tame—love of self, sensuality, power, and material possessions. According to Swedenborg, "they are [our] cravings and appetites" (§45). None of these things are inherently bad. We are created to enjoy food and sex, both of which play central roles in the preservation of the human race. Entertainment is a form of diversion that is important for maintaining our mental health. Money and power are great tools in helping humanity. Love of the self as a vehicle to do good is a very important part of being productive.

But just as wild animals are savage and unpredictable, capable of doing both us and those meeker creatures harm, these self-oriented desires can easily do harm to our love for God and for others. As soon as we fall into the delusion that the goal of life is to serve the self, we become discontent and rapacious; we will do harm to self and others.

In **Day 6,** as a result of our increasing ability to be a channel for the Lord's selfless love, we begin to appreciate sensual and material pleasures and even our very sense of self in a new and deeper way. In the global ecosystem, all species—be they cattle, creeping things, or wild animals—play important roles in maintaining the activity of the whole. We appreciate self as a functional illusion that *allows for* love. We appreciate the special qualities of our bodies, personalities, and their experiences that provide each and every one of us with a unique way of serving life. The fundamental theme of **Day 6,** then, is the wonderful development of our inner desire to do good. We feel the freedom of a heart animated by love for others.

"In the image of God he created them . . ."

Then God said, "Let us make humankind in our image, according to our likeness; and let them have dominion over the fish of the sea, and over the birds of the air, and over the cattle, and over all the wild animals of the earth, and over every creeping thing that creeps upon the earth." So God created humankind in his image, in the image of God he created them; male and female he created them.

(Genesis 1:26–27)

Human beings don't get their own day in the Creation story; we're lumped in with all the other animals. The view of scientific materialism agrees that according to our biological makeup, we are simply animals with complex brains. Likewise, the symbolic meanings of animals and human beings are so united that both are created on the same day. These meanings are uttered in the same breath by Jesus: "'You shall love the Lord your God with all your heart, and with all your soul, and with all your mind.' This is the greatest and first commandment. And a second is like it: 'You shall love your neighbor as yourself'" (Matthew 22:37–39). If animals symbolize love for others, then the creation of human beings represents the development of love for the Lord within our hearts.

Neither of these two loves can exist without the other. To love the neighbor is to love God. As Jesus states: "Truly I tell you, just as you did it to one of the least of these who are members of my family, you did it to me" (Matthew 25:40). To love others is to love the Lord. We don't really love God if we don't love others. Jesus states that we love him to the extent that we follow his commandments: "They who have my commandments and keep them are those who love me; and those who love me will be loved by my Father, and I will love them and reveal myself to them" (John 14:21). And he commands us: "Love one another as I have loved you" (John 15:12). God is infinite selfless love for all human beings, so to the extent that we can love others selflessly, God's life is living within us and through us. We are allowing God's will to animate us, which is to say that we are loving God.

For many years, I vacillated between whether the primary endeavor of life is to love others or to love the Lord. When I was a child, I thought that loving the Lord was most important. Once I became older, though, I saw that God's main message is that we love others and that God can fully take care of himself, whereas people need each other's support. I've come to see that the question sets up a false dilemma; they are so bound together that one cannot exist without the other. I like to visualize the two commandments as a fruit tree: loving the Lord is the tree, and loving others is its fruit. The fruit is the purpose of the tree, but there is no fruit without the tree.

Jesus states that loving the Lord is the first of the two commandments because genuine love for the neighbor flows from love for the Lord. Loving God is loving love itself, which we can do only to the extent that selfishness is quieted. This is why loving God is described as being in his image and according to his likeness—when genuine, it is a selfless love and God is selfless love itself. Our love for God, therefore, is an image and likeness of God. As we will see in the next section, God's love is not an amorphous force; it is that which is truly human.

What It Means to Live One's Life in God's Image

God's creation of humankind symbolizes the development of Christ-like qualities within our spirit. The word *image* refers to vision, which is a more surface quality than what is expressed by the term *likeness*. *Likeness* is derived from the Hebrew word *demuth,* which means "to be like" or "comparable to." There are two fundamental elements of the human spirit that can be aligned with the Lord: our way of thinking and the state of our will. Our minds become truly human when we begin to think thoughts that are congruent with God's way of thinking; and our hearts become truly human when we begin feeling and living out the selfless love that defines the Lord and that he intends for us. Thoughts are more on the surface than are our intentions. When oriented toward selfless love, our thoughts can be understood as images that reveal God, while a loving heart represents a likeness of our loving God. Interestingly, while the Hebrew word that translates into *image* is *tselem,* which means "to carve out" or "to cut," it can also be used to mean "illusion" or even "idol." Understanding spiritual ideas but failing to live by them is an illusory type of faith. Also, when we begin to value our ideas about God more than we live them out, we are worshipping an idol. Even if these ideas are correct, they are lifeless, like a beautifully carved image of God that is nothing but stone. The two, understanding and willing, must go hand in hand. We can't be a true image of God without being a likeness, and we can't be a true likeness without being an image.

To be in God's likeness is to genuinely and humbly desire for everyone's well-being and to therefore serve them accordingly. Human beings are the only part of creation that can know and respond to God and therefore the only part with whom God can have relationship and enter into direct communication. While there are many characteristics unique to human beings that separate us from all other forms of life, only we are able to be raised up above our mere biology into the spiritual realm and into two-way communication with the Lord. Only we are able to look at a tree and see not just the tree but also God's love. We can know oneness. Our capacity to feel deep wonder and awe opens us to experiencing profound gratitude toward the Lord and an appreciation for life. Another reason I follow Jesus is that no other vision of God inspires me with as much gratitude; he became human and suffered as a human to express and share his divine love.

It isn't that we didn't love God before this latter part of **Day 6;** our love for God simply had not matured. Maybe we unconsciously bartered with God, expecting something in return for our efforts at goodness; maybe we were unable to focus on God as a person and instead worshiped a formless spirit or an impersonal source of creation; maybe our devotion was insecure, as we weren't sure whether God truly loved us or whether devoting our lives to the Lord was really the best path for us. At this point in **Day 6,** however, we love the Lord freely, with no strings attached. We just love the Lord.

The Femininity of Divine Truth

There are very few passages in the Bible that offer even a faint glimmer of the Divine as feminine. A few times, the Lord likens himself to symbols of femininity, as when Jesus weeps over Jerusalem, saying how often he "desired to gather [their] children together as a hen gathers her brood under her wings" (Matthew 23:37; Luke 13:34). In Isaiah 66:13, God expresses his love for us "as a mother comforts her child." There is one instance of which I am aware in which Swedenborg identifies God as "the Creatress":

> All human feelings and thoughts arise from the divine love and wisdom that constitute the very essence that is God. The feelings arise from divine love and the thoughts from divine wisdom. Further, every single bit of our being is nothing but feeling and thought. These two are like the springs of everything that is alive in us. They are the source of all our life experiences of delight and enchantment, the delight from the prompting of our love and the enchantment from our consequent thought.
>
> Since we have been created to be recipients, then, and since we are recipients to the extent that we love God and are wise because of our love for God (that is, the extent to which we are moved by what comes from God and think as a result of that feeling), it therefore follows that the divine essence, the Creatress, is divine love and wisdom. (*Divine Love and Wisdom* §33)

This passage from Swedenborg expresses this same idea that we are in God's image and likeness according to our reception of his wisdom (thought) and love (intention). It also, like Genesis 1:27, introduces the idea that the divine, creative essence of God is the very image and source of femininity.

That God created us "male and female" in his own image and likeness is perhaps the most unequivocal statement in the

Bible that women are as equally accurate an image of God as are men and that thus, God is just as much feminine as masculine. This raises the question of why throughout the Bible God is presented—with very few exceptions—only as male.

A symbolic interpretation of the Bible helps shed light on this matter. Since the Bible unfolds linearly as a parable describing the evolution of our spirit, only near the end will our vision of the Lord be sufficiently cleansed of selfishness to be reliably accurate. The stories describe not only our states of mind, but they also express the gradual dissolution of our ego-compromised perception of the Lord. God in the Old Testament is more often depicted as wrathful, while God in the New Testament, Jesus, reveals a more loving God (e.g., rather than stoning sinners, Jesus preaches forgiveness). God doesn't change; it is human perception of God that changes. Given that we see a progressively lucid vision of God as we progress through the Bible, the last two chapters of Revelation in which all things are made new give us the most accurate depiction of the Lord. At the end of the book of Revelation, we read about the holy bride of Jesus who, right along with Jesus and the Spirit, beckons us to come (22:17). That she comes down from heaven, as did Jesus, and that her husband is divine imply divinity. The clincher is that she is actually referred to as holy, "the holy city, the new Jerusalem" (21:2). Only that which is divine is holy.

It is commonly understood that the bride is the church, but what do we mean by *church?* Can any individual or group of human beings be properly described as holy or as descending from heaven? The structure and beauty of the holy city and the rich life that dwells within are given in great detail, and the walls of the city bar all that is harmful from entering.

So we might pose ourselves with a little riddle: What comes down from heaven, is worthy of being described as the holy bride of the Lord, is wonderfully beautiful, and is carefully structured in a way that allows for joy and abundance of life without coming to harm? The only answer can be divine truth. Divine truth alone satisfies these conditions, protecting us from the harm of an ego-driven life. Like the new Jerusalem, divine truth has perfect structure; though we each have a unique sense of selfhood and so have our own vision of divine truth, it is not alterable according to our desires—that is, though we all see her differently, divine truth is her own being, not something we can change.

> The form of heaven that governs all the relationships and communications there is the form of the divine truth, derived from divine goodness, that radiates from the Lord, and we take on this form spiritually by living in harmony with divine truth. (*New Jerusalem* §2)

Divine truth is the bride of divine love, the essential nature of the Lord Jesus, God of heaven and earth. The church is the bride only in the sense that when we allow divine truth from the Word to structure our thinking and our lifestyle, divine love can then dwell within us. Divine truth is brought down out of abstraction and is realized through the human form and through human activity. Only when divine truth has found its home within us can divine love, too, find its home. The two become one within us. This union bears rich fruit in our lives. We serve others and society with wisdom and love.

The truth meant by the new Jerusalem does not merely consist of facts, laws, doctrines, or even understanding—the structural elements of the city. She is also described as the *bride* of the Lord, fully evoking ideas of beauty, love, happiness, and life. The Lord of love cannot be wedded to what is a mere structure, to a form of truth that is void of life. We may memorize the Bible and have a sharp theological mind, but the Lord cannot wed divine love to those facts and insights unless we have a sincere view toward application. Truth becomes alive when we live it out. It becomes responsive to the situations of each moment and so reifies love in the material realm. This perfectly mirrors the way a wife takes in the seed of her husband and turns it into a unique living human being. Each human mind has its own way of thinking, its own way of viewing love, and its own way of manifesting that love.

Therefore, this feminine image of the Divine that is offered in the last two chapters of the book of Revelation represents the union of divine love and truth. Soon after he describes the divine essence as the Creatress, Swedenborg goes on to say that:

> The divine essence is divine love because that love is a property of divine wisdom, and it is divine wisdom because that wisdom is a property of divine love. Because of this oneness, the divine life is a unity as well: life is the divine essence.
>
> The reason divine love and wisdom are one is that the union is reciprocal, and a reciprocal union makes complete unity. (*Divine Love and Wisdom* §35)

So divine femininity is the union of love and wisdom united in life.

The reification of love by means of truth can happen subtly and simply. It can occur in the interactions between strangers on a bus; in the gentle word of a mother to her child; in the way a man loves his wife; in the sharing and cooperation shown by a tight-knit community; or as embodied by great leaders, such as Martin Luther King Jr., who are willing to lay down their lives for the sake of what is right and what is loving.

This truth that is able to realize love in the natural world is wisdom; wisdom is truth that is alive in life. The bride, therefore, is divine wisdom, and the bridegroom is divine love. And the strength of their marriage is made evident by the fact that wisdom that is not full of love is not wisdom, and love that is not wise is not love. As divine love and divine wisdom are united, so there is only one: the Divine. This is why it is never suggested that we worship any form of God but the Lord Jesus Christ. John of Patmos no longer sees the holy city as a bride but is instead participating in her life.

> I saw no temple in the city, for its temple is the Lord God the Almighty and the Lamb. And the city has no need of sun or moon to shine on it, for the glory of God is its light, and its lamp is the Lamb. The nations will walk by its light, and the kings of the earth will bring their glory into it. Its gates will never be shut by day—and there will be no night there. People will bring into it the glory and the honor of the nations. But nothing unclean will enter it, nor anyone who practices abomination or falsehood. . . .
>
> I, John, am the one who heard and saw these things. And when I heard and saw them, I fell down to worship at the feet of the angel who showed them to me; but he said to me, "You must not do that! I am a fellow servant with you and your comrades the prophets, and with those who keep the words of this book. Worship God!" (Revelation 21:22–27; 22:8–9)

So it must be with us. We don't worship the divine feminine; we live it out in our lives. In this way, we, the church, are the bride, or we embody the bride. The essential quality that makes up that bride is divine and not of the illusory self. Nothing of our selfhood is of the bride, but the bride dwells within sense of self. The reason we very rarely see the divine feminine described or depicted in Scripture is that she is lived, not observed. When we look at God, we see truth. When love is united to that truth, we live it out rather than think about it.

The creation of man and woman in God's image is a description of our mind as animated with love for the Lord and with the wisdom that is able to receive that love. Elements of divine truth and divine love did previously give life to our minds, but only now are they fully realized in divine love and wisdom. By fully realized, I do not mean that the fullness of the Divine exists within us, as we are only a small part of the whole. Instead, we are filled fully with the Divine. Our mind and heart together are like a window that needs cleaning. Before it is cleaned, very little light shines through. When it is made spotless, the window realizes its full potential, allowing light to stream in; but the light that it allows is only the minutest fraction of the total light emitted from the sun.

"God saw everything that he had made, and indeed, it was very good."

God blessed them, and God said to them, "Be fruitful and multiply, and fill the earth and subdue it; and have dominion over the fish of the sea and over the birds of the air and over every living thing that moves upon the earth." God said, "See, I have given you every plant yielding seed that is upon the face of all the earth, and every tree with seed in its fruit; you shall have them for food. And to every beast of the earth, and to every bird of the air, and to everything that creeps on the earth, everything that has the breath of life, I have given every green plant for food." And it was so. God saw everything that he had made, and indeed, it was very good. And there was evening and there was morning, the sixth day.

(Genesis 1:28–31)

God's blessing to *be fruitful and multiply* reveals that wisdom and love will increase forever within us. That humans are now to *fill the earth and subdue it* means the Lord's love will reign over all our consciousness. It has taken the supreme position in our spirits, governing our emotions, desires, attitudes, and so our thoughts, words, and deeds: *have dominion over the fish of the sea and over the birds of the air and over every living thing that moves upon the earth.*

Because we are never perfected, God's telling us to *fill the earth and subdue it* can also be seen as a command to intentionally overcome those of our desires and thoughts that are not aligned to the Lord's love. That the vegetation is to be the food for both human beings and beasts explains that our efforts to know truth and to do good are the food that sustains the life of selfless love within us. If we stop putting in effort to be with the Lord, to love others, and to overcome our shortcomings, our feelings of selfless love will languish and expire.

We actually need to have that sense of doing work *as if of self* in order to stay grounded, rooted. Were we to experience only effortless love, the ever-present and ever-necessary sense of selfhood would latch onto it and mistake it as itself in the absence of any evidence to the contrary. The self is kept in subordination by serving the Lord. When the apostles asked Jesus to increase their faith, he spoke a parable, telling of a servant who first works all day in the fields and then, once inside, must work again to cook and serve the meal to the master. Even though the servant has worked hard all day for the master, the master doesn't offer to prepare a meal for the servant. Faith in the master is proven by willingness to work for the master. Tending to the plants that grow in the fields is like the work of **Day 3.** Even after the planting is done, we still have to work to harvest the wheat from the field and make some bread for the master—just as we must still work to feed those higher animations of our spirit, the forms of selfless love that now dwell within us by the mercy of the Lord. While doing this work for the master, we also become aware of our infinite inadequacies, and in this awareness we are steadfast in our humble role as servant. Humility is the foundation of love and wisdom.

SUGGESTED PRACTICES

This chapter describes a state of mind in which we are increasingly animated by the Lord's selfless love—a state resulting from the culmination of all prior states of spiritual evolution. We act *from* sense of self, not *of* self. We are *in* the world, not *of* the world. With the creation of animals, we see the development of our capacity to love others in many "species" of ways. With the creation of human beings, we see the depiction of the development of genuine love for God—for divine, selfless love itself.

Cultivating Awareness in Daily Activities

1

During the **Day 6** period, look carefully at the people you meet, focusing on how each person is an image and likeness of the Lord. Attempt to foster a love of each as such. Try to listen to what the Lord has to say to you through them. This is almost identical to the **Day 4** exercise of looking for the Lord in others. While the purpose of the effort at that time was to gain a sense of the Lord's real presence in our lives, the purpose here has more to do with *loving others* because of the presence of the Lord in them.

2

What animals do you see in your daily routine? Birds? Squirrels? Dogs? Cats? Go on a walk and see what creatures you encounter. Think about what each of those animals might represent on a spiritual level. As there are no coincidences, consider why you might have caught sight of a particular animal at a particular time. Does it help shed light on some aspect of your psychological state? If you want to go deeper, get into a meditative state and then become receptive to the idea that your spirit will bring to your mind an animal that represents something important to you or something that you need to address at this point in your life. Wait and see what happens. If an animal comes to you, try to find out what it symbolizes and what it might mean to you.

Think of your favorite animal. What qualities do you like most about it? What meaning might these qualities have on a spiritual level? If you or someone you know has a pet, consider both its natural and spiritual qualities in contrast with those of animals found in the wild. If you wish, go to the zoo to see its wide variety of animals. What sorts of inner qualities do all of these different types of animals relate to?

Meditative Practice

This meditation will focus on love for others and love for the Lord. Sometimes barriers—such as judgments, resentments, fears, and hurts—inhibit our relationships. This meditation is an opportunity to move through those barriers and enjoy a sense of goodwill toward others and love for the Lord.

I find comfort in the idea that Jesus's infinite love gained victory over and subdued the selfishness that arises from space-time existence. With his mind formed by a love not fettered by space or time, his wisdom was nearly infinite by the end of his life. Therefore, when we pray to him today, because he loved us then, he heard our prayers and was with us. Our love for him now, indeed, may have offered comfort to him as he prayed in Gethsemane. I like to visualize that moment and offer my gratitude to him. Similarly, whenever I am in need of support or just need to make a connection, I sometimes visualize being by the Sea of Galilee, inviting the flesh and blood Lord to meet me there. Somehow this has served as a more meaningful sense of communication than with the Lord as outside of space and time. In this meditation, you will have the opportunity to encounter the Lord in this way. As always, the more deeply you allow yourself to enter into the meditation, the more completely it will promote progress. The more often you meditate, the more lasting its effects will be.

Let's begin with the induction.

[Perform Meditation Induction 2 (p. 59, above)]

Meditation—**Day 6:** Animated by Love

From within this meditative state, spend some time allowing yourself to experience gratefulness for whatever comes to mind. This is called gratitude meditation.

[Pause for about 1 minute]

Now, visualize a loved one as fully and clearly as you can.

[Pause for 30 seconds]

Hold your loved one with gratitude, allowing hope for their welfare to fill your whole being.

[Pause for about 1 minute]

Now, focus on someone that you are experiencing some difficulty with. Visualize them as clearly as possible.

[Pause for 30 seconds]

Allow yourself to wish them goodwill and to hope for their blessing. If you are feeling any animosity or are holding a grudge, allow yourself to enter into the spirit of forgiveness.

[Pause for about 1 minute]

Now, visualize a person that you harbor judgment against—this may be a personal acquaintance; or it may be a politician, a celebrity, or the like. Deeply breathe in the Lord's spirit of forgiveness.

[Pause for 30 seconds]

Deeply breathe in the Lord's spirit of goodwill for this person, seeing them just as the Lord of pure love sees them.

[Pause for about 1 minute]

Now, allow your consciousness to expand out to everyone in your town or city, holding each and every one of them with gratitude and goodwill. Let them become a part of your heart, your being.

[Pause for about 1 minute]

Expand your awareness even further to include everyone on earth, all of humanity. Breathe in the Lord's spirit of love for all, uniting yourself not only with him but with all people.

[Pause for about 1 minute]

Now, imagine yourself kneeling down on the beach of the Sea of Galilee. Let your mind pray that the Lord will be with you, meeting you where you are.

[Pause for 30 seconds]

Visualize the Lord standing before you on the beach. You can see his feet on the sand and feel his hand on your shoulder. Open yourself up to a feeling of adoration and utter gratitude.

[Pause for about 1 minute]

In the quiet that follows, let this scene play out as it will, using this time to be in honest communion with the Lord.

Doing Practice

1

Volunteer some of your time to a charity or to a good cause; or in some other way, give of yourself to either those who are in need or those who will benefit from your aid. Ask the Lord how you might serve him by serving others. If you already volunteer or give of yourself in some way, take the time to consider your motivations, as this may help you gain a deeper understanding of why you do the things you do.

2

Spend time in loving devotion to the Lord. Give God your time and heart.

Suggested Questions for Pondering and/or Discussion

- What was it like to consider others as manifestations of the Lord? Did doing so affect the way you feel about the Lord? If so, in what way?

- Did you find any barriers in your relationship with the Lord? Were you able to overcome them to some degree? How did you do so? What results occurred?

- What insights did you have when considering various animals as representatives of spiritual and psychological realities? Did thinking about the natural and spiritual qualities of animals reveal anything about yourself? If so, what? Did any of these qualities reflect those that you wish to embody or that you admire in others? In addition to asking the Lord for help, how might you develop some of these qualities?

- What thoughts do you have on divine femininity? How could a better understanding of divine femininity have a positive impact on humanity?

- Do you have any further reflections concerning this chapter?

DAY 7: THE SABBATH, THE ONENESS OF BEING

> Thus the heavens and the earth were finished, and all their multitude.
> And on the seventh day God finished the work that he had done, and
> he rested on the seventh day from all the work that he had done. So
> God blessed the seventh day and hallowed it, because on it God rested
> from all the work that he had done in creation.
>
> (Genesis 2:1–3)

In the introduction, we discussed the value of knowing the three elements of any journey: the destination, the path to be taken, and where it begins. The development of our spiritual life is the most important journey that we can ever embark upon. We have seen from where we set out; we have seen an overview of the path we must follow—the effort required and the vistas that we will enjoy; and now, in the description of the Sabbath, we will learn of our ultimate goal, our place of rest.

As has each step in our spiritual development through the Creation story, the Sabbath represents a state of mind. At the beginning of Genesis 2, we are told that *God blessed the seventh day,* which means that the Sabbath is a state of blessedness, a day of peace and rest from labor. That the description of the seventh day is not included with the other six days in Genesis 1 but instead begins Genesis 2 suggests a distinction between this day and the others. During **Days 1** through **6,** we are working from ideas *toward* a state of love; but on **Day 7,** we are working *from within* a state of selfless love. This blessed peace arises as our will, thoughts, and actions become aligned and start to flow with the universal current of divine love. It is the difference between fighting upstream against the current of our worldly life and becoming one with that divine river.

When the intelligent, human, all-loving God has accomplished within our spirits all the work of **Days 1** through **6,** we are ready to experience **Day 7.** Similar to the parallels between **Days 1** through **3** and **Days 4** through **6,** there is an interesting connection between **Day 7,** the day of rest, and **Day 0,** the state before spiritual evolution begins. In **Day 0,** it can be said that we exist along the stream of self-love without resistance—that's how blind we are to divine love. In **Day 7,** we are at rest because the spirit of divine love animates us and bears us along its flow like a leaf upon a river. Also, because our spiritual evolution is perpetual, each arrival at a Sabbath state gives birth to a new influx of light to begin the process again in a new facet of our life. In infants, we see the holiness of an undivided consciousness. Spiritual evolution can lead a person to have a similarly undivided mind in which there is peace and loving acceptance. The former state arises from ignorance, the latter from wisdom.

In the Sabbath state, we feel a sense of oneness with God, with life, and with others. **Day 7** is the peace of oneness. Our mind has become a home in which selfless love resides. Since our mind is alive with the divine love that is now able to flow into us and out to others, we are given to experience oneness with the Lord, fulfilling the wish of his final, fervent prayer before his trial and death—that we might all be one:

> As you have sent me into the world, so I have sent them into the world. And for their sakes I sanctify myself, so that they also may be sanctified in truth.

I ask not only on behalf of these, but also on behalf of those who will believe in me through their word, that they may all be one. As you, Father, are in me and I am in you, may they also be in us, so that the world may believe that you have sent me. The glory that you have given me I have given them, so that they may be one, as we are one, I in them and you in me, that they may become completely one, so that the world may know that you have sent me and have loved them even as you have loved me. (John 17:18–23)

As there is only one God, and God is selfless love, to experience selfless love as the animation of consciousness is to feel union with the Lord. Thus, the marriage of divine love and wisdom within our minds, which is what is meant by the creation and union of man and woman, leads to a state of mind that becomes wedded to the Lord's selfless love. We have reached our destination. We are embodying the bride in this Sabbath state.

This state also describes our union with others and with nature. Since divine love and wisdom are present within all of God's creation, when our mind is alive with God's love, we see its manifestation not only in others but also in all other life around us. We recognize that this one divine love unites all life.

Experiencing the Lord's selfless love as that which animates our mind allays fear. Selfless love evaporates resentment and dissipates all self-desire. In the absence of fear, hostility, and desire, we discover peace. Our eyes are opened to see that all is refulgent with divine glory. Our spiritual eyes are seeing through our natural eyes. The Spirit of God is in and expressed by each and every thing we see. No longer some nebulous entity that exists out beyond our sensible perception, God now pervades our being and can be sensed in all that is around us. And we know deep down that all is well because God is omniscient, omnipotent, and all-loving. All is held by God.

The Sabbath is a state of mind in which the self-based will has been quieted to make room for a new, living will that is characterized by a love for the Lord, a love for other people, and a love for life. The Lord has furnished us with a new heart, one that is attuned to the Lord's divine selfless love. To the extent that we understand divine love as having nothing to do with the illusion of selfhood, we are given to experience this love as if it was our own will. Just as a great teacher's love of a subject, and of her students, is able to inspire them to also love that subject, God has made his will our will. Our desire to be loving without any strings attached, inspired by God, has been fulfilled by God.

Far from being demotivated by the realization that a personal ability to love is illusory since all is an expression of divine love and wisdom, we find that we are more proactive and alive than ever before. We are full of spontaneous, responsive love that allows us to live our life in the fullest possible way. Unlike **Day 4,** which is a life-changing first-personal encounter with God that impresses upon sense of self, **Day 7** represents a gentle state into which we have evolved over time by slow, continuous dissolving of faith in self. Since we reach our destination by a process of evolution, the intensity of heightened awareness does not burn us out as it can in our **Day 4** encounter.

When the Lord has imbued our sense of self with his selfless love and our will with his will, there is no more antagonism between ego and the Lord. We are more productive than ever, and yet we do not feel as if we are expending psychological effort or energy. Rather than laboring against old ego-based habits and delusions, we are now simply letting the divine river flow through us. As the *Tao Te Ching* so aptly describes it, we work without working. We are in harmony with God's will and so with life as it presents itself to us, and this brings about a tremendous state of psychological restfulness.

This state of oneness with God is the highest state we can experience, the oneness of being. The name of God, Yahweh, speaks of the truth that God alone has being and so *is*. The primary duty of Muslims is utter submission to God so that one's will is replaced with God's. In the Hindu tradition, we hear Krishna's words to Arjuna: "Get up and prepare to fight. After conquering your enemies you will enjoy a flourishing kingdom. They are already put to death by My arrangement, and you . . . can be but an instrument in the fight. . . . Simply fight, and you will vanquish your enemies." These enemies can be understood as symbols for the enemies within, the deluded desires and thoughts of a self-orientation. And the central tenet of Buddhism is that individuality is illusory and that *mukti,* freedom, and *nirvana,* the final goal, are characterized by a state of oneness.

In **Day 4,** when we first encountered the Lord in a personally meaningful way, we necessarily had a taste of this oneness of being, enough to soften the delusion of self and pave the way for the days to come. The **Day 4** state, however, is fleeting, as it clashes with all we've ever known from within the delusion of self; the Sabbath state, on the other hand, is long-lasting and all-encompassing. Subsequent to **Day 4,** one of our major hurdles is the desire to pursue spirituality and a more intimate relationship with the Lord in order to experience heightened emotional states. The ego assumes the throne, masquerading itself as something holy in pursuit of something holy. In **Day 7,** we are no longer seeking these emotional experiences that come with loving others and the Lord; we are seeking simply to love the Lord and to love others, without ulterior motive. Some versions of the Sabbath state are not as distant or lofty as they may seem. When we are immersed in some activity that we thoroughly love and that is useful, we enter *flow* states of mind. Athletes enter *flow* states when they so enter into the playing of the game that there is no room for other thoughts. The love

of the game, which has value to society and so contains something of divine love, flows through them and animates them.
Musicians experience this, as can accountants and research scientists, when they lose track of time and self-reflection due to
absorption into their work. Anyone can experience this when
they are performing any valuable service.

While **Day 7** is our destination, it is by no means the end.
The self becomes ever quieter as it does the work of each of the
prior six days, but we will have to perpetually go back and do
that work in order to keep ourselves spiritually grounded; we
must always be the servant and never assume the role of master.
In fact, **Days 1** through **6** are all present within the Sabbath.
Each day lays the foundation for the next so that the entire
story might be visualized as a spiral of development. We might
also visualize the Sabbath as a hanging fruit, within which the
sun, the life of the tree, the soil, and all the decay within the
soil are present. Notice, too, that while a Sabbath state might
evolve in relation to overcoming one particular temptation
(e.g., anger), we may not necessarily evolve to that state in relation to our work on another of our sins (e.g., greed). In fact,
across the many aspects of our sense of selfhood, all seven days
of spiritual development can be occurring simultaneously. Evolution is a constant, multifaceted endeavor.

Were we never to revisit earlier stages, we would think of
ourselves as finished or perfected; and this would clearly lead
to an inflated sense of self. Swedenborg describes witness-
ing a process that angels undergo to address such a situation.
When angels begin to forget that it is not they who should be
credited for the goodness in which they live, they are let down
into egoic states of mind as a means of having them recognize
that all credit is due to the Lord, and they are then lifted back
up into a heavenly state of mind (*Divine Providence* §79:3).
Also, "by . . . alternations of delight and discomfort, [angels']

perception of and sensitivity to what is good become more and more delicate" (*Heaven and Hell* §158).

In **Day 6,** we looked at the bride, or the holy city described in Revelation, as divine wisdom, that of the Divine which is expressed as femininity. In **Day 7,** we are now living inside the holy city, the new Jerusalem. Our mind has become structured in accordance with the city's design, fortified against danger by its walls and wedded to the Lord's divine love. Before our experience of oneness with the Lord, we feel as though we are *apart from* the Lord; once we have this experience, though, we feel ourselves as *a part within* the Lord's life. On **Day 7,** we are now full *part*icipants of the Divine.

Swedenborg uses a term that translators convert to the English phrase *love to the Lord.* The actual Latin means "love into the Lord." I am not sure why this is, as I see it, consistently mistranslated. Perhaps *love into the Lord* doesn't readily make sense. However, when we consider that the evolution of love within our lives increasingly unites us with the Lord, *love into the Lord* makes perfect sense. We are ever entering deeper and deeper *into* divine life.

SUGGESTED PRACTICES

This chapter describes the inner peace and oneness we experience when we become an open vessel for God's selfless love as a result of the God-driven evolution of spirit that takes place during **Days 1** through **6.**

Cultivating Awareness in Daily Activities

How does one enter into that place of peace known as the Sabbath? What can we *do?* Mindfulness and meditation can create states in which we have a diminished sense of self, experience oneness with God and life, and have an increase in feelings of goodwill toward others. Such states offer a taste of the

Sabbath, but in the absence of continual work on self-improvement and efforts at blessing others, these states are ephemeral. Remember, too, that we can experience something of Sabbath states when we become fully immersed in our work or useful recreation.

Ultimately, it is all the work of **Days 1** through **6** that creates the fertile ground out of which the state of oneness with the Lord can grow. Therefore, the task for this chapter is to simply continue doing the work of the prior chapters. Go through and pick the three or four practices that were most beneficial to you, and then focus on those again during the **Day 7** period. Regardless of which exercises you choose, beneath it all, you can always make efforts at being present and focusing deeply on humbling yourself before the Lord.

Meditative Practice

Meditation helps suspend the ego, and suspending the ego helps us to gain a taste of the state of oneness—oneness of mind and oneness with others, with life around us, and with God. We enter into the oneness of being. Gaining such a taste is good because its sweet peace spurs us on in the journey. Meditation has also been proven to provide a wide range of benefits for mental and even physical health. Among these are increased empathy and an increased sense of tranquility.

After following the initial imagery, you will be asked to unite your breathing with the image of the Lord. In this meditation, we are experiencing the reality of God's spirit flowing in, through, and out of us. You are invited to simply be a part of the breathing, the words, and the flowing of spirit, without separating any of the components, including your selfhood.

Let's begin with the induction.

[Perform Meditation Induction 2 (p. 59, above)]

Meditation—**Day 7:** The Sabbath, the Oneness of Being

From within this meditative state, allow your mind to become deeply absorbed with the following scenes.

Light falling on water . . .

[Pause for 15 seconds]

Sunlight streaming through the clouds . . .

[Pause for 15 seconds]

A powerful tree with strong roots and a wide-spreading canopy of beautiful branches . . .

[Pause for 15 seconds]

The radiant yellow sun in a vast azure sky . . .

[Pause for 15 seconds]

The silver moon in a clear night full of stars . . .

[Pause for 15 seconds]

Fish moving through flowing waters . . .

[Pause for 15 seconds]

White birds gliding across the sky . . .

[Pause for 15 seconds]

A deer standing in a lush forest . . .

[Pause for 15 seconds]

The face of a loved one . . .

[Pause for 15 seconds]

The shining figure of God . . .

[Pause for 15 seconds]

Holding the image of God in your mind, repeat the following mantra with each breath, entering the meaning of the words as fully and genuinely as you can so that the thought and the act become inseparably one: Breathing in, say to yourself, "In, Lord . . ." Breathing out, say, "Thank you, Lord . . ."

[Pause for 1 minute; then read the following]

From John 17:

After Jesus had spoken these words, he looked up to heaven and said, "Father, the hour has come; glorify your Son so that the Son may glorify you, since you have given him authority over all people, to give eternal life to all whom you have given him. And this is eternal life, that they may know you, the only true God, and Jesus Christ whom you have sent. I glorified you on earth by finishing the work that you gave me to do. So now, Father, glorify me in your own presence with the glory that I had in your presence before the world existed. . . .

"All mine are yours, and yours are mine. . . . I am not asking you to take them out of the world, but I ask you to protect them from the evil one. They do not belong to the world, just as I do not belong to the world. Sanctify them in the truth; your word is truth. . . .

"I ask not only on behalf of these, but also on behalf of those who will believe in me through their word, that they may all be one. As you, Father, are in me and I am in you, may they also be in us, so that the world may believe that you have sent me. The glory that you have given me I have given them, so that they may be one, as we are one, I in them and you in me, that they may become completely one, so that the world may know that you have sent me and have loved them even as you have loved me. Father, I desire that those

*also, whom you have given me, may be with me where I am,
to see my glory, which you have given me because you loved
me before the foundation of the world.*

*"Righteous Father, the world does not know you, but I
know you; and these know that you have sent me. I made
your name known to them, and I will make it known, so
that the love with which you have loved me may be in them,
and I in them."*

[Pause for 1 minute]

ooooo

In the quiet that follows, breathe in and out slowly and
deeply.

Doing Practice

One thing that the Lord did on the Sabbath was to heal. It may
seem a tall order to heal others, but to be in a Sabbath state is
to be a healer. Swedenborg describes how love for the Lord
gives rise to love for others, which in turn assembles all our
ideas and perceptions into proper order, the order of heaven.

> When truth is arranged in the same pattern that charac-
> terizes heaven, it is in the heavenly pattern and gains en-
> trance to goodness. Truth and goodness display this pat-
> tern in every angel and are being arranged in this pattern
> in every human who is being reborn. To sum up, the heav-
> enly pattern is the pattern in which the truth espoused
> by faith is arrayed within the good embraced by charity
> for one's neighbor, and in which charitable good is arrayed
> within the good embraced by love for the Lord. (*Secrets of
> Heaven* §4302:3)

Try focusing on loving the Lord as you make efforts to love others. As you do so, you will increasingly see God in others and in all life around you. You will find the inner peace of the Sabbath state and you will be a healer.

Suggested Questions for Pondering and/or Discussion

- As this is the conclusion of **Day 7,** you may wish to take this opportunity to review the experiences and observations that you have had since beginning this journey. What was most beneficial? What was most surprising? What was most difficult?

- What are some of the Sabbath states that you have experienced? How have they affected your life?

- Which aspects of your journey do you most wish to carry forward with you after this day of rest? Why?

- How has your vision of or relationship with the Lord changed? In what ways do you think it will continue to change?

- Do you have any further reflections concerning this chapter or any of the previous chapters?

CONCLUSION

At the beginning of this book, I suggested some criteria to be met for the symbolic interpretation of the Bible to be plausible. The first criterion was that the symbols made sense—that when the meaning of a symbol was explained, the mind would readily consent to its sensibility. The second criterion was that when the interpretation of these symbols was arranged in the order presented in the Bible, there would be a consistent sequential meaning. Both of these criteria have been met: the meanings of the symbols make intuitive sense, and they remain consistent throughout the interpretation. As when the waters of **Day 2** were revisited in **Day 5** and the vegetable life of **Day 3** was referenced in **Day 6**, the meanings of these symbols fit seamlessly into the pattern of days described at the beginning of **Day 6**. A smooth and coherent sequential meaning is also presented, wherein each day leads naturally to the spiritual characteristics described in the subsequent days. Indeed, there could be no other order for the development of the spiritual states of mind described. The third and final criterion was that these symbolic meanings yield valuable fruit that can be applied in our lives. The inner meaning of each day of Creation provides us with insights into both our psychological and spiritual natures, into the Lord's nature, and into how he evolves us. Each day also offers practical ideas about how we can more actively participate in the process of our spiritual evolution by means of our sense of selfhood. Crucially, the Lord actually evolves us through his very description of our evolution; learning about the process catalyzes the process. In other words, the Word of the Lord speaks us to life. An obvious example of this is in reading about the Lord's self-sacrificial love in the Gospels. If we allow ourselves to really *read* the story, it is incredibly moving—sad and beautiful at the same time. We can't help but be inspired to love Jesus, and in loving him, we are inspired to emulate him and also to do what he suggests—love others as he has loved us. That's the power of the Word.

The book I wrote several years ago, *12 Miracles of Spiritual Growth,* focused on this idea. Each healing miracle performed by the Lord, when read carefully, has the power to perform a parallel or corresponding miracle in our psychological and spiritual lives. The healing of the blind man in John 9 stands out to me. In searching for meaning in that story, I felt like I was seeing in ways where once I had been blind—namely, that all that is is ultimately for the glory of God, and when I don't perceive it that way, it is due to self-based judgment.

In the seven days of Creation, learning about what each day means helps propel us. For example, learning about how the natural mind is born in a state of spiritual darkness and devoid of genuine love shines some spiritual light into our lives, and we have therefore been moved forward to **Day 1.** Learning more about spiritual light and vision then opens the door for us to start thinking about higher and lower thoughts, **Day 2.** Once we read about, ponder, and observe these higher and lower thoughts, we become motivated to seek a spiritual life, which is what **Day 3** is all about. The Word of God does to us what it describes, and so in this way, it authors us to the extent that we are devout and sincere in our effort to understand its meaning.

I have felt this happen multiple times in my life, and it is always wondrous. It is this process that I understand in the words from Psalm 62:11–12:

> Once God has spoken; twice have I heard this: that power belongs to God, and steadfast love belongs to you, O Lord. For you repay to all according to their work.

AN AFTERTHOUGHT

Now that we have explored our spiritual evolution as described in Genesis 1, I would like to briefly explore the physical evolution of the natural universe, because the meaning we discover there will offer a wonderful complement to our understanding of spiritual development.

Establishing the Connection

Scientific materialism would explain that there is no spirit and that things such as emotions and intentions are merely the results of chemical and electrical events within the brain. According to this view, a merely physical, biological machine can function only by the mechanical laws of cause and effect by which the physical universe operates; and any event that breaks the rules governing the cause and effect of the physical realm must necessarily lie outside of that realm.

There may be physical evidence of the nonphysical, or spiritual, giving rise moment by moment to physical reality. Quantum phenomena seem to lie outside of discernible hard laws of physics and can be understood only in terms of probability. Some have offered that this may explain consciousness, will, and choice. Since quantum phenomena operate outside of the physical realm, then by definition they are *super*-natural, which is to say nonphysical, events. The term *quantum mechanics,* therefore, is misleading, as the events are *not* explained by mechanical laws. Scientists are unable to pinpoint actual physical mechanisms that govern quantum phenomena, which suggests to me that our understanding of reality cannot be confined to what we know as the physical realm. So in this case, the constant emerging of the building blocks of substance would mirror the *Secrets of Heaven* quote at the beginning of this book, which says that the spiritual creates and sustains the physical universe moment by moment.

A purely material view of evolution also gives rise to a logical problem in relation to consciousness. If all is governed by mechanical cause and effect, including our emotions and intentions, then it stands to reason that a subjective sense of consciousness is not possible, let alone necessary, within such a strictly physical reality. The view of scientific materialism states that the human organism is governed only by the mechanical laws of physical reality. If we are nothing more than cogs within a mechanical universe, then we could just as easily navigate our environment, eat, and procreate without sentience. In a merely physical reality, there is no value in sentience. What's more, anything locked within a mechanical cause-and-effect system is not able to have self-awareness. A spinning fan will never come to understand it is spinning. A robot can mechanically navigate, but because it is governed by cause and effect, it will never have what we understand to be consciousness. Consciousness requires a perspective that lies outside of the events it is observing. If consciousness is a product of those events, it cannot also observe them.

In his book *The Selfish Gene*, Richard Dawkins—a genetic biologist and proponent of atheism—describes humans as lumbering puppet-slaves animated by DNA, the function of which is to reproduce itself by means of the human form. I had to be very meticulous in how I worded that last sentence. I almost used the phrase *DNA that seeks to reproduce itself* and then considered the phrase *designed to reproduce itself,* but both of these phrases indicate will and purpose, which are things that cannot exist in a merely mechanical, physical realm. I can't help but wonder how a purposeless universe would produce a chemical that not only reproduces itself but in the process creates magnificent, conscious life. Why bother with reproduction at all? Even the idea of selfishness implies will. If there is nothing but mechanics, then there is no will, and consciousness requires will and emotion. Imagine having no will and no sense of delight or joy. We would have no drive to think or do anything, which means that we would have no consciousness. Our will cannot arise from the mechanical laws of cause and effect. So, if will were somehow programmed into us, it would indicate a programmer and therefore a purpose outside the mere random mechanics of a lifeless realm.

Though not a deist, I believe we can learn a great deal about the realm of spirit and the Divine through careful meditation on the physical realm. Swedenborg offers that the natural universe speaks a secret language describing God and the nature of the spiritual realm. So the more that science discovers, the more we learn about God. To establish a little ground on the relationship between the Divine and the natural world, it can help to take a general tour of the natural universe and its creation from the scientific perspective.

A Universe Most Grand, Beautiful, and Mysterious

The story of our universe begins an estimated 13.8 billion years ago with a very small point of stuff. *Very small* is rather an understatement. Imagine the earth no bigger than a grain of sand. Now imagine a grain of sand upon that miniscule earth. Now imagine *that* grain of sand as another earth. A grain of sand upon *that* earth might provide at least a vague idea of the smallness of the singularity that gave birth to the universe we know and love today. It is believed that this ridiculously miniscule point suddenly expanded to be a million billion miles wide within the first minute after the inflation began and that within the first second of expansion all the known forces of physics came into being.

Throughout the progression from the tiniest fraction of a second after the birth of the universe until the present moment, we see a pattern of organization repeated over and over again, forming long, branching chains of events through time, each link of which depends upon the former in an amazing series that climaxes with human consciousness in this tiny corner of the universe. Quarks join to quarks to form protons; protons join to electrons to form hydrogen; hydrogen binds with hydrogen in massive balls of nuclear fusion to form radiant suns where helium is created. Some of these suns become incredibly powerful supernovas that fuse subatomic particles together to give birth to all of the more massive elements within the universe. These elements in turn coalesce to create worlds. On one such world, Earth, life began.

At each step, we see smaller, less meaningful entities joining together to become more meaningful, substantial, and influential gestalts (organized wholes). In so doing, the unities of the lesser parts are effectively more real than are the parts when separated. An isolated quark is more or less nothing, possessing no meaningful size, weight, charge, or ability to interact with matter. If a particle exists in the woods and there is no other particle to interact with it, does it still exist? But quarks united with other quarks give rise to both charge and mass, and therefore they are able to have meaningful influence and relationship with the stuff of our universe. Thus, the union of quarks is effectively more real than individual quarks in isolation. Likewise, electrons and protons have no meaningful size when isolated. But when joined together, their union occupies a space that is hundreds of thousands of times larger than that of the proton and millions of times larger than that of the electron and so is, again, effectively more real in terms of area than when the two particles are separated. Their union creates the functional reality of space and substance, which before were nonexistent. Similarly, when hydrogen atoms bond in nuclear fusion, from out of the cold, dark silence burst forth unfathomable amounts of energy. Each step of the unfolding universe involves unions, and each union creates gestalts of a more meaningful, substantial, interactive, and dynamic nature. Because of these new qualities, we can say that the union of the parts is effectively more real than each of the individual parts.

The same pattern where parts unite to form much more meaningful wholes continues beyond the creation of the elements. Four common elements—carbon, hydrogen, oxygen, and nitrogen—combine in various ways to create amino acids, which are often called the building blocks of life. Among these nonliving chemical compounds, there are twenty that unite in various ways to form the many hundreds of thousands of different proteins needed for life to exist. These proteins don't occur outside of living things. On average, a protein involves a chain of about two hundred amino acids joined together in a unique and necessary order. There is no known reason why amino acids would become assembled in any specific order at all. The odds of a specific two-hundred-amino acid protein coming into being spontaneously are one out of a number that has 260 zeroes.

Those are worse odds than we have of winning the Powerball—a lot worse. In order to win in the lottery of life, you'd have to do better than pick the one winning atom from all the atoms in the entire universe! To put it in perspective, there are more suns within the universe than there are grains of sand on earth, and each sun contains an incomprehensible number of atoms. But actually, the odds of life are worse even than that—

much, much worse. The odds described above are of the creation of just one protein consisting of a chain of two hundred amino acids; but as mentioned, life requires many hundreds of thousands of such proteins. Some proteins involve strings of more than a thousand amino acids, thus making the odds of our existence so unlikely that human imagination simply cannot fathom them. It would be like picking the one winning atom from all atoms existing within millions of universes.

Some have suggested, including Richard Dawkins, that these proteins didn't assemble instantaneously but that they evolved. Regardless of how proteins came to be, they are incomprehensibly unlikely. Yet before we even get to the unlikely probability of the specific makeup of a protein, we must realize that the union of amino acids to form even a single protein is also inexplicable. From within a merely physical framework, it shouldn't have happened at all. Amino acids, as monomers, have never once been observed joining together to form polymer proteins.

But, despite all odds (and I do mean all!), life began, carrying on the same pattern that we have seen repeated from the beginning of time: less meaningful pieces joining together to create a more meaningful whole. And as for biology, we've just begun. Proteins are neither alive nor able to reproduce themselves. Without deoxyribonucleic acid (DNA), the proteins that sustain life would become extinct. But DNA has no purpose in and of itself. It, too, is not alive. There is nothing about the chemical sequence of DNA that makes it especially adapted to surviving in the sea of chemicals that make up physical reality. In fact, DNA is supremely elegant and unlikely. It is hard not to reach the conclusion that DNA exists for the sake of reproducing proteins. But when we begin to use terms like *for the sake of,* we are implying purpose.

Up until this point in our "tour," for the sake of unbiased observation, I have worked hard to avoid implying that there is purpose within natural reality, because purpose implies a goal to be achieved; and a goal can be had only by an intelligent and willful being. But the facts all but force us to use the language of purpose. DNA exists *for the sake of* reproducing proteins. And since it must exist before the intelligent, willful beings of biology can exist, it is not irrational to entertain the real possibility that there is a purpose within the universe, that is, a goal. And if there is a goal, or direction, within the unfolding of the universe, there must be an intelligent and willful being causing the universe to be as it is.

And even this is not the full story. The relationship between protein and DNA requires a third partner, ribonucleic acid (RNA). Without RNA, no reproduction of protein can occur. The greater the number of components that cooperate for a single purpose, the more difficult it is to assume a random cause. And remember that each of the three components is nonliving and entirely unlikely in and of itself.

The story is yet even more wondrous. DNA, RNA, and proteins can't cooperate to make life unless they are in a protective home, a cell. The components of a cell are uncountable. There are an estimated one hundred million protein molecules in each cell alone. Each component and each organized structure within a cell is miraculous in itself. And yet none of these components are alive in and of themselves; they sustain life only when together. Thus, each aspect of a cell has meaning only in relation to every other aspect of that cell. Why would nonliving chemicals join together as a cell? How are they capable of doing so? It is as if they *wished* to live. Can nonliving chemicals have desire of any kind at all? Obviously, they can't. And if we assume that they in fact do not desire anything, how and why did nonliving material assemble into such unimaginably unlikely and complex relationships that form the container of life? In the words of the humorous and eloquent author Bill Bryson, the formation of a cell "is rather as if all the ingredients in your kitchen somehow got together and baked themselves into a cake—but a cake that could moreover divide when necessary to produce *more* cakes. It is little wonder that we call it the miracle of life."

Throughout the entire history of the universe, we see the same pattern on all levels: lesser entities assembling together in such a way as to become something more meaningful than any of their constituent parts. What better definition for love can there be than individuals joining together to serve a higher and more beautiful purpose than living for one's self? That is a precise definition of love, and that is what we see throughout all levels of the universe and throughout its entire history.

The assembly of less meaningful parts into a more meaningful gestalt is suddenly much more astounding when we see that nonliving matter comes to house or embody life. The very basic bacteria cells that first manifested as life in turn had to undergo some amazing unions and transformations to create much greater beings. All animal cells are actually the necessary union of two dissimilar life forms. Within each and every cell in all humans and animals live mitochondria, which are very tiny independent life forms with a genetic makeup foreign to that of their host cells. Without this endosymbiotic relationship between the cell and its mitochondria, we would not exist.

Similarly, plants rely on the existence of chloroplasts within their cells, which are also indwelling foreign life forms. And without plants to provide oxygen, humans and animals would not exist. And without humans and animals to provide carbon dioxide, plants would become extinct. Therefore, the animal and vegetable kingdoms unite as a mutually interdependent whole. Again, there is this fractal of gestalts forming an inextricable web of reality. We might call this the "pattern of patterns."

The most simple and elegant explanation for what we see throughout the universe and its history is a God whose fundamental nature is love. The pattern we see is the very definition of selfless love: the kind of love most, if not all, religions describe as the fundamental nature of the Divine. The physical universe is an ever-opening revelation of God. Since this progressive evolution of the universe is an expression of God, it is logical to deduce that we will experience a similar evolution within our spirits, which is the topic of this book.

Single cells containing mitochondria began to join together to form, among other things, you and me. I hardly need to make an argument for the awesome construction that is the human body. Take any organ in isolation, and you will see unfathomable order, and each organ works only in union with one another to form us.

And what exactly are we? We don't generally feel like a gathering of cells or even organs; we have no sensation of the workings of the kidneys, liver, or pancreas, to name a few. We sometimes notice the stomach and the intestines, and though we can easily notice the heart and the lungs, we typically observe them from a third-party perspective, without their being part of the sensation of selfhood. Even the seat of our consciousness, the brain, spins away without us knowing firsthand anything at all about how it works, which suggests that consciousness is something grander and fundamentally other than the constituent parts of our body from which it arises. Our very being is a great mystery, and yet here we are: consciousness riding within a vehicle composed of ten trillion endosymbiotic cells, each consisting of precise and purposeful assemblies of nonliving chemicals. What is truly awesome, in the deepest sense of that word, is that our minds are therefore cradled upon the entire history of the universe. From the Big Bang onward and outward in a spreading tree of life, all has transpired to culminate in you and me in this very moment (which happens to be the moment you are reflecting on this fact). The universe is noticing itself.

The atoms were doing just fine without us; they were existing on their own. The chemical compounds were likewise in no fear of ceasing to exist, yet they assembled to form life. And these unicellular bacteria were in no jeopardy for millions of years; nevertheless, they assembled to form much more meaningful beings, including you and me. There are observable mechanisms that explain some of the steps in this process. Gravity and nuclear fusion, for example, are responsible for the creation of chemical compounds; and the theories of evolution and epigenetics account in broad strokes for the successively more complex rise of life. But there are still huge gaps in our understanding of how a singularity at the beginning of the universe evolved into what we are.

Even if we were able to fill in all these massive gaps, there is still a nagging question that begs to be answered: Why? If natural reality has no purpose, underlying meaning, or direction, why do things occur the way they do? What is the purpose of survival? Why would a gene want to reproduce itself? Why does a lion protect her young? Why did chemical compounds get together and form a cell in the first place? Why does gravity exist as a uniting force? And most significantly, why do we see the same pattern of gestalts repeated over and over again, not only throughout the history of the entire universe but also on all levels within the universe (the subatomic, the elemental, the chemical, the biological, the ecological, and the social)— independent components always assembling to create unities whose greater meaningfulness and interactivity make them more alive and so more real than the components?

What I am arguing is that even if science could explain every last one of the massive gaps in the progression from the singularity to human consciousness, it still could not answer the question of *why*. Knowing how something works does not explain *why* it exists or *why* it works the way it does. Thus even if our scientific knowledge was perfect, the possibility of an intelligent and purposeful Author remains strong.

There is a strange twist in the thinking of many people that results in an unseen double standard. Let's imagine that a person asks, "Why does an apple fall?" Most people would reply, "Gravity." But in fact, gravity is not really an explanation at all. *Gravity* is just a word we use to describe something we don't understand. We know what gravity does; Sir Isaac Newton discovered (later refined by Albert Einstein) mathematical laws that predict its activity, but who is prepared to say why gravity attracts or why it exists in the first place? Even if a gravity particle is discovered, we will still know no more about how or why this particle works than we do about gravity as it is known today. Similarly, we know what an electrical charge does and so can harness it, but nobody knows why it exists or why it does what it does. Gravity, electricity, and the like are means, not causes.

Science is great at explaining *how* things work, but sometimes we are fooled into thinking that it answers the question *why*, the question of cause. Cause cannot be understood by scientific thought; it can only be understood in terms of purpose, value, and function. As soon as we begin to consider the intrinsic value of something, we are assuming its purpose. And as soon as we assume purpose, we assume intelligent and will-based direction. We have now moved from the arena of science to the realms of philosophy and religion. In a subtle form of circular logic, scientific materialism raises science up as the only source of truth; and since science cannot answer the question *why*, it assumes there is no answer to the question, and so we learn to stop asking *why*. I see an ostrich with its head in the sand, thinking to itself, "If I can't see it, it doesn't exist." In a way, it is more sinister than this. It is as if we are confined within a box and don't even realize we've been imprisoned, so we don't know to seek a way out.

But those who take a hard and honest look will not only recognize their imprisonment but also begin to see that there is something beyond. Before Bryson offered his cake analogy (see pages 201–2, above), British astronomer Fred Hoyle (1915–2001) similarly noted that the random creation of life would be as likely as a tornado flying through a junkyard and spontaneously assembling a jumbo jet, which suggests an intelligence at work. Richard Dawkins countered this implication by saying that to assume there is an intelligent Creator behind such an unlikely event leaves us with an even more unlikely event. To have created, the Creator would have to be more complex and intelligent than the creation. Dawkins's point is that saying God created everything leaves a mystery—the mystery of how God came to be.

An analogy can help us here. Imagine that human beings begin exploring Mars and find a sphere that has an entrance with a closeable door. Once inside, they discover the ways in which the object functions: By pulling certain levers, it can rise and move through the air at lightning speed. Like the Internet, the sphere has a store of seemingly infinite knowledge and is able to do all manner of calculations. It is extremely elegant and designed in such a way that if any one piece were out of place, the sphere would no longer function.

The obvious conclusion is that some sort of intelligent being created this sphere. Its elegance, its functionality, and the interdependence of its parts all point to purpose and intelligent design. In fact, it is designed to allow another intelligent creature to use it. Though we cannot see the aliens and are left wondering about their nature and origin, we would be fools to deny that aliens created the sphere and instead assume it came to be without any purposeful Creator. Similarly, the most simple and reasonable explanation for the marvelous progression, order, functionality, elegance, delicate interdependence, and beauty within the universe is that it is created by an intelligent Author.

The beautiful, bountiful order within and throughout the natural universe binds simple and less meaningful things into communities that give rise to more meaningful and vital things; and this points not just to an intelligent creator but also to a loving one. Every aspect of the natural universe is a depiction, description, and definition of love. Even chaos, characterized by the occurrence of seemingly random events, is governed by very elegant laws of design. Though we can't explain the nature and origin of an Author, all evidence points to there being loving, intelligent authorship. Though we can't explain how Martians came to exist or why we can't see them, the sphere itself reveals strong evidence of intelligent authorship.

A more fundamental problem with Dawkins's question of *what caused God* is that it is bound within space-time, when God, by definition, is outside of space-time. Time is a paradigm, or pattern, that puts a limitation on complete knowledge. Human consciousness is bound within any given moment of time, but that doesn't necessarily mean that other moments of time don't simultaneously exist. In fact, scientists recognize space and time as making up a single continuum. When I am in the bedroom, the living room is still real. Likewise, who is to say that when I am in today, tomorrow doesn't already exist? The fact that tomorrow always "arrives" is strong evidence that it does indeed exist today. Most physicists are quite convinced that the arrow of time (the experience of time moving in one direction from past to future) is a limitation of the human mind and not an inherent property of the laws of physics. They cannot explain mathematically or even hypothetically why time shouldn't flow backwards. Furthermore, time is liquid according to the state of mass and movement in space. Time, space, mass, and energy are ultimately one entity; it is our perception that divides these things.

Any question that is based on a fallacy leads to a fallacious answer. So, asking about cause based on our fallacious perception of time will not do. Let's not ask about the ultimate cause *in* time, as Dawkins baits us to do. Let's instead investigate a cause that lies outside of time. As we have seen, that the universe evolves according to a recurring, fractal pattern points to the idea that all natural events are the effects or reiterations of one reality. All effects contain the entire chain of causality and so contain within them the whole of reality. Instead of thinking of cause and effect in time, we can think of cause and effect as one intrinsically united whole, fully and always present right here and now. In other words, there is no cause and effect; there is simply one eternal reality that is being itself. Each moment in time is a recapitulation or re-presentation of that singular reality. Reality as viewed by minds bound by space-time, therefore, is the continual self-revealing of a single entity. Our experience of reality results from our space-time-bound mind existing in and moving through that which transcends and is therefore wholly present in all space and all time. In short, limited consciousness leads to perception of finite reality. We are seeing a part of the Infinite, when we think we are seeing what is finite.

We arrive at the conclusion, then, that the prime cause of reality is inherent within reality itself. If there is a God, a divine source and prime cause of all reality, then that divinity cannot help but be present and expressed within all moments of time, all events, and all entities. And, therefore, if there is a divine prime cause outside of time, any failure to observe that divinity is a failure in consciousness. So in response to Dawkins's question of *what came before God* or *what caused God*, the answer is that the question doesn't make sense. God Is. Temporal cause and effect are only meaningful within finite consciousness. The Hebrew word for this divine presence within all reality is YHWH: I AM WHO I AM. Alternatively, this could be interpreted as I AM BEING or simply as I AM. We can catch a glimpse of having perception of God outside of time by focusing on the here and now as holy.

Consider that there is a divine being outside of space-time who causes this reality in terms of its being and nature. In order to help us see how this might function, we can imagine this divine being as a sphere and space-time reality as a two-dimensional plane. The sphere cannot be contained by the plane, but the plane can exist within the sphere. Now let us imagine that the sphere desires to reveal itself within the context of the plane, and so from one end of its being to the other, the sphere moves through the plane. Because the plane is created in and of the sphere, it exists only as successive cross-sections of the sphere. The order, nature, and intelligence of the sphere would be manifested as spontaneous orderly patterns arising within the plane. We can compare this to the successive cross-sections of the magnetic resonance imaging (MRI) of a brain—patterns emerge and change in relation to each other. If we played a video of the sequentially emerging cross-sections to an unsuspecting individual, he or she would assume that each cross-section caused the one subsequent to it by virtue of the observed pattern. But the truth is that while each cross-section is indeed related to the ones previous and subsequent to it, no one cross-section causes any other.

Citizens of any cross-section of the sphere would understand their reality as having suddenly appeared as a tiny point out of nothingness. This point would for inexplicable reasons suddenly and rapidly expand. From within the plane, they would notice spontaneous patterns and order arising from unknown sources. They would also presume a cause-and-effect relationship between one moment, or cross-section, and the next. They could not help assuming such relationships. They would even be able to predict some of the grosser aspects of the future, due to the observance of repeated patterns. They would not, however, understand the concept of a sphere, because it transcends the limitations of their mind and senses. But they *may* be able to guess that there is something beyond their vision of reality that is creating and ordering this vision. This is startlingly similar to our perception and current understanding of the universe: a singularity, an unimaginable inflation or great expansion, the arising of pattern and order as if out of nothing and for no apparent reason, the assumption of cause and effect within the boundaries of the dimensions we perceive, and the speculation that an intelligent being not bound by our space-time limitations is the source of all that is.

Our senses and forms of logic are greatly limited by the dimensions of space-time. We would be very arrogant to assume that there was nothing beyond what the mind and senses can ascertain within natural reality. It is quite rational to assume a reality that is transcendent of the physical. Each moment is a container and expression of the prime cause, which is not a cause within space and time but one that is transcendent of them. This prime cause is represented to us in a very limited translation known as *space-time*. To believe in the Divine is supremely rational, and it is sad that scientific materialism has blinded us to believe that all we sense with the body is all that's real. Given the pattern of love, which is the perpetual growth toward order and beauty that we witness in the universe, it is rational to assume that God is pure divine love and that each moment is holy.

It could be suggested that an even more real and intelligent entity beyond God causes God in the way in which I suggest God causes space-time. But this question would continue *ad infinitum*, and we would be left with an infinite regression of more and more real entities. I am reminded of certain Hindu paintings in which the face of a deity is repeated in all directions like a peacock's tail, infinitely outward. And I am also reminded of the fact that many modern theoretical physicists wonder if there isn't a whole host of universes that function like membranes. When these universes contact one another, yet another universe is created—cosmic procreation, if you will.

Even within an infinite regression of universes, though, we still see an overarching pattern that is mirrored again and again in each iteration of reality. This pattern of patterns remains the same, which suggests that the pattern of patterns is more real than any one version of the pattern. The overarching pattern of patterns has a simple and elegant explanation: the pattern of patterns is ultimate reality and the source of all; in a word, it is God. The pattern we see in the universes—lesser entities binding to create more real and functional unities—is more real than the vehicles that house the pattern. So, we can truthfully say that the pattern of patterns is more real than the universes that house it, because the pattern's dominion is evidenced within the universes but unexplained by the universes themselves. Therefore, the infinite regression of universes and transcendent causes is passive, and the pattern is active.

The pattern is love. Divine love is the Creator and is the I AM of all that is. This pattern has deep implications for our purpose as individuals and as the human race. As is all else in the universe, we are designed to unite with one another in love to create a better and effectively more real organization. In fact, we see this occurring all the time. From universities to sports teams to governments to NGOs to churches to families, we achieve much more as groups than we do as individuals—often for the sake of good. In marriage, two come together and create a new, wondrous being, and family is created. Just as we saw different parts joining together to serve different functions within a whole at prior stages in the evolution of the universe, we see the same today in human organizations. Based on the chain of events that led up to our existence, I would even go so far as to say that it is our destiny to inevitably unite as a human whole and fulfill our ultimate purpose.

We are a part of the ever-opening revelation of divine love that is the universe. Human consciousness is the most recent iteration of these leaps from parts to a new gestalt, and the human mind is able to both love selflessly and reach far beyond the confines of space and time. For these reasons, as human beings, we are a closer approximation to God than anything else we know of. We are made in God's own image and likeness. The human body, therefore, will offer us a powerful window into the divine nature. We can learn about the Divine by learning about the nature of the human body. This lends credence to the idea that the Divine is better understood as human than as something nebulous or other than human. This is a truth found in the gem of Hindu texts, the *Bhagavad Gita,* and in Jesus's words to Philip in the Gospel of John, "Whoever has seen me has seen the Father" (14:9).

In human society, we each serve in specialized ways, just as different cells participate in different organs. Some of us are pillars of society—strong, upright, morally pure, traditional—and can be compared to bones—strong, upright, and structure-providing. Yet just like inflexible bones, the pillars of society can sometimes be judgmental and unyielding. Then there are those of us who resemble muscles—those who like to get practical things done to advance society. Some of us are like the circulatory system, primarily concerned with reaching out to others with love. Such people are able to love everyone regardless of their flaws, just as the heart sends blood to all cells. Uniquely, red blood cells lack nuclei, which can be seen as symbolic of those people who have become selfless and are therefore dedicated to meeting others where they are and as they are, without judgment.

We as individuals reveal one tiny aspect of God—each person uniquely reflecting certain qualities of God more strongly than other qualities. Society needs all types, and it is in our togetherness that we best reflect the Divine. God's personhood is fully and simultaneously all of these aspects: he is the bones, pure and strong; he is the heart, selflessly loving, endlessly giving, causing his life-giving rain to fall equally upon the wicked as it does upon the good; he is the musculature motivating the progression of all that is good in our lives and of the entire physical universe; he is the All within all; he is I AM. Not only can the human body help us to understand society and the many aspects of God's personhood, but it can also help us to understand the nature of our own spirits, which are reflections of God's nature.

BIBLIOGRAPHY

Bhaktivedanta, A. C. *The Bhagavad-gītā as it is*. NY: Collier Books, 1972.

Bryson, Bill. *A Short History of Nearly Everything*. New York: Broadway Books, 2004.

Buber, Martin. *I and Thou*. New York: Simon & Schuster, 1996.

Dawkins, Richard. *The Selfish Gene*. Oxford: Oxford University Press, 2016.

Nicoll, Maurice. *The New Man: An Interpretation of Some Parables and Miracles of Christ*. Baltimore, MD: Penguin, 1972.

Swedenborg, Emanuel. *Apocalypse Explained*. vol. 6. West Chester, PA: Swedenborg Foundation, 1997.

———. *Divine Love and Wisdom*. West Chester, PA: Swedenborg Foundation, 2010.

———. *Divine Providence*. West Chester, PA: Swedenborg Foundation, 2010.

———. *Emanuel Swedenborg: The Universal Human and Soul-Body Interaction*. New York/Mawah: Paulist Press, 1984.

———. *Heaven and Hell*. West Chester, PA: Swedenborg Foundation, 2010.

———. *New Jerusalem*. West Chester, PA: Swedenborg Foundation, 2016.

———. *Posthumous Theological Works*. West Chester, PA: Swedenborg Foundation, 1996.

———. *Revelation Unveiled*. New Century Edition. West Chester, PA: Swedenborg Foundation, Forthcoming.

———. *Secrets of Heaven*. vol. 1. West Chester, PA: Swedenborg Foundation, 2010.

———. *Secrets of Heaven* (1749–56). Unpublished section translations by Lisa Hyatt Cooper. §§4302:3; 4353:3; 6056; 6057:1–2, 3; 6058; 9683:1, 2.

———. *True Christianity*. vol. 1. West Chester, PA: Swedenborg Foundation, 2010.